DISCOVERING THE LEADER IN YOU

WORKBOOK

DISCOVERING THE LEADER IN YOU
WORKBOOK

Sara N. King

David G. Altman

JOSSEY-BASS
A Wiley Imprint
www.josseybass.com

Center for
Creative
Leadership
www.ccl.org

Published by Jossey-Bass
A Wiley Imprint
989 Market Street, San Francisco, CA 94103-1741—www.josseybass.com

Readers should be aware that Internet Web sites offered as citations and/or sources for further information may have changed or disappeared between the time this was written and when it is read.

Limit of Liability/Disclaimer of Warranty: While the publisher and author have used their best efforts in preparing this book, they make no representations or warranties with respect to the accuracy or completeness of the contents of this book and specifically disclaim any implied warranties of merchantability or fitness for a particular purpose. No warranty may be created or extended by sales representatives or written sales materials. The advice and strategies contained herein may not be suitable for your situation. You should consult with a professional where appropriate. Neither the publisher nor author shall be liable for any loss of profit or any other commercial damages, including but not limited to special, incidental, consequential, or other damages.

Jossey-Bass books and products are available through most bookstores. To contact Jossey-Bass directly call our Customer Care Department within the U.S. at 800-956-7739, outside the U.S. at 317-572-3986, or fax 317-572-4002.

Jossey-Bass also publishes its books in a variety of electronic formats. Some content that appears in print may not be available in electronic books.

Library of Congress Cataloging-in-Publication Data

King, Sara N.
   Discovering the leader in you : how to realize your personal leadership potential / Sara N. King, David G. Altman, Robert J. Lee.—New and rev. ed.
      p. cm.—(A joint publication of the Jossey-Bass Business & management series and the Center for Creative Leadership)
   Earlier ed. entered under: Robert J. Lee.
   Includes bibliographical references and index.
   ISBN 978-0-470-49888-0 (cloth); ISBN 978-0-470-90225-6 (ebk);
   ISBN 978-0-470-90228-0 (ebk); ISBN 978-0-470-90230-2 (ebk)
1. Leadership. I. Altman, David G. II. Lee, Robert J., 1939- III. Lee, Robert J., 1939- Discovering the leader in you. IV. Title.
   HD57.7.L439 2011
   658.4′092—dc22

                                                                         2010032373

Discovering the Leader in You Workbook: ISBN 978-0-470-60531-8 (paperback);
ISBN 978-1-118-10350-0 (ebk)

Printed in the United States of America

FIRST EDITION
PB Printing   10   9   8   7   6   5   4   3   2   1

A Joint Publication of

The Jossey-Bass

Business & Management Series

and

The Center for Creative Leadership

CONTENTS

PREFACE

The best leaders are committed to continually improving themselves and others in their organization and community and to undertaking a leadership journey that is an ongoing, dynamic process without a clear beginning, middle, and end. Whether you are currently a leader or aspire to a leadership position, this workbook will help you take that journey by providing a systematic process for discovering who you are as a leader and making more conscious choices about why, when, how, and where you lead.

This workbook is based on concepts in CCL's best-selling book, *Discovering the Leader in You, New and Revised Edition*. Although you do not have to be intimately familiar with the book to benefit from the workbook, we recommend that the impact will be greatest if you obtain copies of both the book and the workbook. You might want to read the book before starting the workbook; after you finish the workbook, you can use the book to explore areas that you would like to develop.

LEARNING OBJECTIVES

When you complete this workbook, you will be able to:
- Clarify your purpose for leading, based on a clear leadership vision and a core set of values
- Articulate your leadership strengths and areas for development
- Understand who you are as a leader in the context of both your work and personal life

- Determine when and why you feel unclear or stuck in your leadership journey
- Develop, use, and monitor an action plan for becoming the best leader you can be

If you have objectives that are not listed above, write them here:

_____

_____

_____

ABOUT THE WORKBOOK

Each of the seven chapters of the workbook except Chapter One, which establishes the context, and Chapter Seven, which helps you pull everything together, has the following sections:

- A brief introduction to set the stage
- "What's in This Chapter?"—a quick preview of the chapter content
- "Learning Objectives"—what you will accomplish by doing the activities in the chapter
- "Your Current State"—questions and activities that help you focus on where you are now in relation to the topic
- "Explore the Topic"—questions and activities to help you reflect on, think through, assess, and articulate your experiences, thoughts, ideas, and perspectives
- "Expand Your Learning"—additional questions and activities that require more time and, often, the input of others
- "Themes and Patterns"—questions and activities to pull together what you have learned and reflect on what it means in terms of your leadership journey
- "Now What?"—questions and activities to help you think about how you will use what you have learned
- "What's Next?"—a brief preview of the next chapter

Here's an overview of the chapter topics:

- *Chapter One: Where Does Leadership Fit in Your Life?* Sets the context for the workbook by helping you think about where you are now as a leader; explains the concept of drift, which can derail even otherwise successful leaders; and describes the Discovering the Leadership Framework on which both the workbook and the book are based
- *Chapter Two: Organizational Realities, Demands, and Expectations.* Examines the importance of understanding trends in organizational life and their impact on you as a leader, differing perspectives on leadership, and the potential costs of leadership
- *Chapter Three: Your Leadership Vision.* Helps you develop a clear, compelling leadership vision that is connected to your personal vision and can clarify your actions and choices
- *Chapter Four: Your Leadership Motivations and Values.* Provides insights into the motivations and core values that drive your leadership
- *Chapter Five: Your Leadership Profile.* Helps you explore the personal styles, competencies, responses to change, and work experiences that have an impact on your leadership and the leadership choices that you make
- *Chapter Six: Personal Realities, Demands, and Expectations.* Examines key factors, demands, needs, and expectations in your personal life that influence and shape your leadership
- *Chapter Seven: Action Planning.* Helps you pull together everything that you have learned, develop an action plan for moving forward, and consider the implications of what you have discovered for future decisions you make about your leadership

ABOUT THE ACTIVITIES

This workbook includes a variety of questions and exercises to help you think about, examine, explore, and discover concepts and issues related to yourself as a leader. You can complete most of the activities while you are going through the workbook; others require more time, and some involve other people. So that you can get the most out of the workbook, we encourage you to do all the activities, do them thoughtfully, and be as honest as you can with yourself throughout the process.

KEEP A LEADERSHIP JOURNAL

To expand your learning, we encourage you to keep a leadership journal, both while you are completing this workbook and as you continue on your evolving leadership journey. Your journal might be a notebook that you carry around with you or a file on your laptop or mobile electronic device. Use it to record your thoughts, ideas, and observations. Leadership development is an ongoing process, and keeping a journal can be an important part of that process.

WORKING WITH OTHERS

Although this workbook is designed so that you can go through it on your own, people often find that the leadership journey is more rewarding when they work with others. Here are some suggested ways to reap the benefits of working with others:

- Go through the workbook with a coach or mentor who can help guide you through the activities and serve as a sounding board.
- Meet informally with colleagues who are going through the workbook to discuss the concepts and activities and give one another feedback.
- Use the workbook in a formal class or training program.

BEFORE YOU BEGIN

To prepare for the work you are about to do, consider these questions:

1. People become leaders in many ways: for example, by assuming a formal leadership position; assuming an informal leadership role; being asked to take on

a leadership role; or volunteering to be the leader in a specific situation. If you are already a leader, how did you become a leader? Also, briefly describe your current leadership role.

_____

_____

_____

_____

_____

If you are not currently in a leadership role, describe one or more times when you have been in a formal or informal leadership role in the past. For example, have you been a manager or supervisor in an organization? Led a task group or committee? Coached a soccer team? Chaired a volunteer association board?

_____

_____

_____

_____

_____

2. Your attitude toward developmental experiences shapes those experiences. Take a few moments to think about how you feel about the development process in general and going through this workbook in particular. Which of the following statements most closely describes your feelings?

- ☐ I enjoy developmental opportunities such as this one. They offer a pleasant break from my routine.
- ☐ I welcome the chance to learn more about myself and how I can be more effective in my work. I am prepared to focus my attention and energy on this workbook.
- ☐ Although I can understand the benefits of this type of development, it takes time and energy away from my important work.

If you checked the first or second box, you're ready to begin. If you checked the third box, you may want to come back to the workbook at a time when your workload is more conducive to making an investment in a development process.

We wish you much success in your journey to discover the leader in you!

DISCOVERING THE LEADER IN YOU
WORKBOOK

CHAPTER ONE

WHERE DOES LEADERSHIP FIT IN YOUR LIFE?

People become leaders in many different ways and for many different reasons: some actively seek leadership roles; others are asked to take on such roles; still others become leaders organically, by informally assuming leadership positions in various situations. But no matter how you become a leader, it is and will continue to be critical to make conscious choices about why, when, how, and where you lead.

The ability to be clear about the choices you make will help you avoid the problem of drift that every leader experiences at one time or another: doubts about your capabilities as a leader, questions about how best to leverage your talents, or confusion about the leader within you. Drift can feel as if you are going through the motions but not actually moving forward. It can leave you unable to make conscious choices and take action with a clear sense of purpose that is connected to your values and goals.

WHAT'S IN THIS CHAPTER?

This chapter includes:

- The Discovering Leadership Framework: An overarching framework that will help you connect who you are as a leader with the realities of your organizational context and personal life, providing you with the awareness that you may need to find your way out of drift and avoid it in the future by being clear about choices that are important to you

- Questions and activities to help you assess what you already know about your current situation and what leadership means to you

LEARNING OBJECTIVES

When you complete this chapter, you will be able to:

- Articulate the underlying reasons that you are a leader now or aspire to be a leader in the future
- Identify whether you are in a state of drift and, if so, identify possible causes

THE DISCOVERING LEADERSHIP FRAMEWORK

The systematic framework on which this workbook is based (Figure 1.1) is designed to help you connect who you are as a leader (your vision, values, and profile) to the realities of both your organizational context and your personal life so that you can better match your talents to your opportunities.

The Discovering Leadership Framework addresses five key topics:

1. *Current organizational realities.* What is the situation in which you lead? Every leader functions in a specific organizational context. That context is affected by current social, economic, global, and industry trends, as well as situational factors in the leader's organization and role. To avoid or address the problem of drift, you need a good understanding of the broader circumstances and the demands and expectations that affect you as a leader.

2. *Leadership vision.* What is the role that leadership plays in your life? Being purposeful about what you want in life is crucial to being purposeful about what you want as a leader. A clear, compelling leadership vision is essential for evaluating your leadership choices.

3. *Leadership values.* What are your values—the standards or principles that guide your beliefs, decisions, and actions? Understanding your values and leveraging them as a cornerstone of your leadership choices may give you more insight into why you feel adrift.

4. *Leadership profile.* Who are you as a leader, and what do you bring to your leadership role? Your leadership profile can include many things, such as

FIGURE 1.1 Discovering Leadership Framework

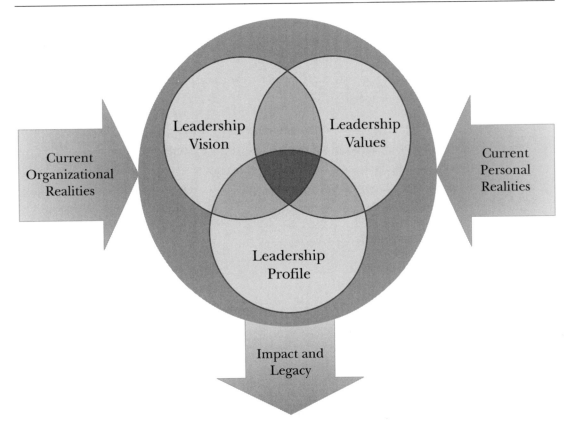

your competencies, styles, and experiences. Analyzing your profile will give you a good understanding of your strengths and developmental needs.

5. *Current personal realities.* What impact do your personal and work lives have on one another? Many leaders tend to compartmentalize those two areas of their lives when they would benefit by thinking about them in a more integrated and holistic way. After all, you are one person whether you are at work or at home.

Addressing these five topics will help you determine the impact you have as a leader and the legacy you will leave.

YOUR CURRENT STATE: WHERE ARE YOU NOW?

Where are you now on your leadership journey? The questions and activities that follow will help you articulate your current perspectives and assess your current relationship to leadership.

1. Write three to five sentences that express why you want to be a leader. What do you want to accomplish through your leadership? What do you see as your overarching purpose as a leader? If you are not sure that you want to be a leader, write a brief statement that explains why you aren't sure and what you think is contributing to your uncertainty.

_____

_____

_____

_____

_____

2. Following are some reasons that leaders experience drift. On a scale from 1 to 5, with 1 being very little (a low level of drift), 5 being very much (a high level of drift), and N/A meaning "does not apply to me," rate the extent to which each of the following factors is affecting you right now:

I feel overwhelmed with too much responsibility.

       1   2   3   4   5   N/A

I am skeptical about the long-term success of changes in my organization.

       1   2   3   4   5   N/A

I feel stuck because I see little chance for advancement in my current position.

       1   2   3   4   5   N/A

I am no longer excited about my job.

       1   2   3   4   5   N/A

I feel lost and unsure about whether I can handle some of the responsibilities I have been asked to take on.

1   2   3   4   5   N/A

I am in denial about the challenges I face and cope by trying to ignore the changes that keep coming at me.

1   2   3   4   5   N/A

I feel angry because I have to leave my current job, which I love, and I don't know how I will find the next leadership role.

1   2   3   4   5   N/A

I am unhappy because my job does not seem to be connected to my core values.

1   2   3   4   5   N/A

I feel pressured because my financial needs mean that I must serve in a high-level, high-paying position that is tremendously demanding.

1   2   3   4   5   N/A

I feel underchallenged because I think that I can handle more responsibilities than my boss seems willing to give me.

1   2   3   4   5   N/A

I am worried about how I can take on more responsibilities than I already have, considering all the demands in my professional and personal life.

1   2   3   4   5   N/A

I am thrilled because I have just landed my first real leadership role, but I am unsure about how best to organize, lead, and motivate my team.

1   2   3   4   5   N/A

I am nervous because I am about to take on an extremely challenging leadership position that will chart new territory, and I am not sure what to do first.

1   2   3   4   5   N/A

Review your responses. Remember that high numbers represent high levels of drift. What trends do you see? Then summarize your current state of drift.

_____

_____

_____

_____

_____

3. How would you currently evaluate your strengths and weaknesses as a leader? For example, are you a good communicator? Do you demonstrate integrity? Do you excel at delegating, building teams, or developing others? Can you build trust with a wide range of people? Are you adaptable? Innovative? Comfortable with change and ambiguity? Do you have technological savvy? Are you good at building networks and alliances? Do you know how to lead in a global context?

In the left-hand column, list three to five skills and competencies that you consider strengths. In the right-hand column, list three to five skills and competencies that you think you need to improve.

Strengths   **Need to Improve**

_____   _____

_____   _____

_____   _____

_____   _____

_____   _____

Briefly describe how your weaknesses might be getting in your way.

_____

_____

_____

Briefly describe how your strengths help you in your current role.

_____

_____

_____

EXPLORE THE TOPIC

The questions and activities in this section will help you explore the concept of drift and take a closer look at your desire to be a leader. They will also help you determine whether you are in a state of drift and, if so, what might be contributing to your feelings of drift.

We learn a lot from observing others. Try it yourself. Answer the questions below about leaders you know about or know personally:

1. Think of a person who appears to be driven to lead by a clear purpose that resonates highly with you. This can be a famous person you have read or heard about or someone you know quite well.

What do you think this person's purpose for leading might be?

_____

_____

_____

What makes this person's purpose compelling?

_____

_____

_____

In what ways is having a clear purpose related to this person's effectiveness as a leader?

_____

_____

_____

What behaviors do you think characterize someone who leads with conviction?

_____

_____

_____

2. What about a leader who doesn't have a clear purpose (or has not communicated his or her purpose in ways that you can understand)? What are the implications for this leader's effectiveness?

_____

_____

_____

3. Now think about a leader you have known personally for at least a few years and who you think is currently in a state of drift. What do you think the possible causes of drift could be for this person?

_____

_____

_____

If you were this person's mentor or coach, what advice would you give him or her about getting out of a state of drift?

_____

_____

_____

4. Mihaly Csikszentmihalyi (1990) describes "flow" as times when you are so absorbed in an activity that you lose your sense of time and place. Recall yourself at two different times in your leadership journey: a time that you were in a state of drift and then a time where you were in the flow.

If you could have coached yourself when you were in a state of drift, what advice would you have given yourself?

_____

_____

_____

What lesson can you take from the time when you were in the flow that might be useful when you are in a state of drift?

_____

_____

_____

5. Sometimes drift happens because you are not in a role that capitalizes on your strengths. Therefore, you need a good understanding of what you do well and what you need to improve. Use the following activity, adapted from *Leadership Wisdom: Discovering the Lessons of Experience* (Wei & Yip, 2008), to gain insight into your strengths and needs.

The list that follows contains some of the key characteristics that leaders need in today's competitive, fast-paced, global world. Use the rating scale to indicate how well each statement currently describes you.

A = Always   S = Sometimes   N = Not usually

———————   I can draw on both rationality and intuition in making decisions.

———————   I am comfortable with ambiguity.

———————   I am open to multiple perspectives.

———————   I weigh the consequences of alternatives.

———————   I clearly see the right course of action among multiple conflicting priorities.

———————   I have a good understanding of my own personal strengths, limitations, and emotional status.

———————   I have a good understanding of the personal strengths, limitations, and emotional status of others.

———————   I recognize my own emotions and manage them effectively.

———————   I recognize the emotions of others and manage them effectively.

———————   I am good at building strong and supportive relationships with different types of people.

———————   I am people oriented, and my values are based on collective well-being, not on my own gains.

———————   I model the way and align my actions with my words.

———————   I focus on tasks and results.

———————   I am willing to experiment to make changes happen even when facing uncertainties and challenges that are complex and stressful.

What are some insights you gained from your responses to the items on the checklist? What characteristics might you want to develop further, and how might you go about developing them?

_____

_____

_____

_____

EXPAND YOUR LEARNING

The following activities can help you learn more about your purpose for being a leader and any feelings of drift you may be experiencing. Note your observations and responses to the questions in your leadership journal:

1. To help you expand your thinking, show the statement that expresses why you want to be a leader to a few friends, family, or colleagues, and ask them for their thoughts, reactions, and questions.

2. Take a quiet moment to think about your purpose for becoming a leader and where you want to be as a leader in the next three years. Write down the first three words or phrases that come to mind. Then use a search engine such as Google Image Search to find an image that represents your response. (As an alternative, you can look for images in a magazine such as *National Geographic*.) Briefly describe that image and how it connects to your vision and purpose in your journal.

3. Now think about where you are right now with respect to being in a state of leadership drift. Write down the first three words or phrases that come to mind and search for an image that represents your response. Briefly describe that image in your journal and its connection to your feelings of drift.

4. Looking at what you wrote, think of some actions you could take to move from a state of drift toward where you want to be as a leader in three years.

THEMES AND PATTERNS

Use the following questions and activities to pull together what you have learned in this chapter about drift and the underlying purpose driving your desire to be a leader:

1. Having done the activities in this chapter, how clear would you say you were about the purpose that drives your desire to lead and the factors that might be causing you to drift?

My purpose in leading: ____Very clear ____Somewhat clear ____Not very clear

The factors that cause me to drift: ____Very clear ____Somewhat clear ____Not very clear

2. Ernest Hemingway was once challenged in a bar to write a very short story. He wrote the following six words: "For sale. Baby shoes. Never worn."

Try it yourself. Reflect on your responses to the questions in this chapter. Then write a six-word story that expresses what you have learned in this chapter about purpose and drift. (As an alternative, write six words that summarize the major takeaway points or learning from the chapter.)

_____   _____   _____   _____   _____   _____

3. What other insights have you had from this chapter?

_____

_____

_____

_____

_____

4. Writing a letter can be a useful process for summarizing your thoughts. Write a one- to two-paragraph letter to yourself about the topic of leadership drift and purpose that does the following:

- Articulates your reasons for wanting to be a leader
- Explains whether you think you are in a state of drift and, if so, what the reasons might be

LETTER TO MYSELF

_____

_____

_____

_____

_____

_____

_____

_____

_____

_____

NOW WHAT?

What will you do to use what you have learned in this chapter? Which actions can you take immediately? Which actions require the help of others? Whose help do you need? What can you do to get it?

Action	Can take now? Yes or No?	Requires help from	To get help, I will

What do you still need to explore and understand about drift and the underlying purpose of your commitment to leadership?

_____

_____

_____

_____

_____

WHAT'S NEXT?

In the next chapter, you will examine the organizational realities and trends that have an impact on you as a leader.

CHAPTER TWO

ORGANIZATIONAL REALITIES, DEMANDS, AND EXPECTATIONS

External forces, as well as your organization's culture, have an impact on you as a leader. Trends in your work life affect the leadership opportunities available to you, what is expected of you as a leader, and what you can accomplish. At times, changing organizational realities and expectations can lead you to think, *Is being a leader worth it?* An understanding of your personal leadership situation can help you answer that question.

Leaders must constantly define and redefine their leadership skills and perspectives to meet the demands of such organizational realities as increased competition, economic downturns and upturns, reorganization and mergers, changed organization-customer relationships, new definitions of careers and work, workforce diversity, globalization, rapid technological innovation, and more. Leaders who can be flexible and innovative and can adapt well to change are more likely to be successful and less likely to find themselves in a state of drift.

Not only are organizations constantly changing to meet the demands of a changing environment, there is no longer only one perspective on leadership. Instead of being identified by job title or description, leaders can emerge at any time and in any context, and there are differing views about how a leader should lead. For leaders, those differing perspectives can result in unclear, even conflicting, expectations and demands. Successful leaders need a good understanding of their own view of leadership, as well as the ways in which their organization rewards certain leadership styles or philosophies.

The demands and expectations that result from changing trends and perspectives can have both high costs and high benefits. An understanding of what those costs and benefits are for you can help you develop strategies to keep costs from hindering your success while taking advantage of opportunities that come your way.

WHAT'S IN THIS CHAPTER?

The questions and activities in this chapter will help you:
- Understand how specific current trends affect your organization and your role as a leader
- Articulate your view of leadership in the context of your organization
- Recognize the ways in which your organization rewards certain styles or philosophies of leadership
- Identify the demands inherent in your leadership situation, assess their costs, and develop strategies for dealing with those costs

LEARNING OBJECTIVES

When you complete this chapter, you will be able to:
- Describe specific organizational dynamics (trends, culture) that influence you as a leader
- Identify your primary view, perspective, or philosophy of leadership
- Identify the specific costs of leadership that might be contributing to your leadership drift

YOUR CURRENT STATE

This section will help you see what you currently know about the organizational realities, demands, and expectations that affect you as a leader and about the costs of leadership to you.

1. What are some of the key external challenges currently facing your organization or team? The key internal issues it currently faces? Describe them briefly.

(If you are not part of a formal organization, think of community, civic, religious, or school groups that you belong to.)

Key external challenges:

_____

_____

_____

_____

_____

Key internal issues:

_____

_____

_____

_____

_____

2. Think back over the past year or two. What organizational or team changes have had significant impacts on how you do your work and accomplish your goals?

_____

_____

_____

_____

_____

3. What kinds of leaders are supported, reinforced, and rewarded in your organization or team? What are leaders rewarded for doing or not doing?

_____

_____

_____

_____

_____

Thinking about the kind of leader you are and what leaders are rewarded for doing or not doing in your organization or team, how would you rate your fit with the organization?

_____Excellent fit _____Very good fit _____Good fit _____Adequate fit
_____Poor fit

4. What do you find the most difficult about your current leadership role? Check all that apply:

☐ Long hours

☐ Insufficient resources

☐ Not enough staff

☐ Too much diversity among staff

☐ Too hard to retain and motivate staff

☐ My boss's management style

☐ Other

☐ Too much travel

☐ Too-frequent or too-abrupt change—or both

☐ Unclear, contradictory, or unreasonable expectations

☐ Increased customer demands

☐ Too much rapidly changing technology

☐ Frequently changing formal or informal organizational policies

5. Do you think you were right to choose the leadership path you are on right now? At this moment, how would you answer this question: Is leadership worth it? Then briefly explain your answer.

_____Yes, definitely   _____Yes, most of the time   _____Not sure

_____No, not usually   _____Definitely not

EXPLORE THE TOPIC

The questions and activities in this section will help you identify and assess relevant trends and perspectives in the organizational context that affect your leadership, identify your philosophy of leadership, and identify the costs to you of changing demands and expectations.

Note: You might need to do some research before you answer the questions in this section.

1. Trends in the external environment affect organizations and, by extension, leadership in those organizations. Examples of some trends follow. Check those that significantly affect your organization and thus you as a leader. Add any relevant trends that are not in this list.

_____Higher competition   _____Labor costs moved offshore

_____Technological advancements   _____Decentralization

_____Economic downturns   _____Globalization

_____Health care reform   _____Increases or changes in
government or industry regulations
_____Other external trends that
currently affect my organization

_____Other (specify):

_____Other (specify):

_____Other (specify):

2. Check the organizational issues or changes that follow that currently affect you in your leadership role or are likely to affect you during the next year or two. Briefly describe the issues or changes and the ways in which they are affecting or will affect you as a leader. Add any relevant items that are not listed.

_____Restructuring   _____Redefinition of job

_____Boss retirement   _____Recent promotion

_____Shared resource pool   _____Merger with another organization

_____Reduction in staff   _____New CEO, executive director, or president

_____Introduction of new product line   _____Outsourcing

Other organizational issues or changes that affect or are likely to affect you as a leader:

_____

_____

_____

3. Leadership culture can be defined as the values, beliefs, and assumptions about how people work together that reflect the organization's collective approach to achieving direction, alignment, and commitment. Which of the descriptions that follow most closely reflect the culture of your organization? Check each of these.

Dependent culture

☐ Decision-making authority is concentrated among a few people in specific positions of responsibility.

☐ One's measure of success in this organization comes primarily from the boss's assessment.

☐ My contributions to this organization do not require me to know much about how my work relates to that of other groups and departments.

☐ Fitting in and respecting tradition is a valued quality in this organization.

☐ Leaders in this organization are fairly conservative in their approach to change.

Independent Culture

☐ One's measure of success in this organization comes primarily from success in achieving challenging performance targets.

☐ Ambition is a valued quality in this organization.

☐ Bold and independent action that gets results is highly prized in this organization.

☐ Even during major change, leaders here exert great pressure not to let performance numbers go down.

☐ People in this organization operate under the philosophy that it's better to ask forgiveness later than it is to ask permission first.

Interdependent Culture

☐ My contributions to this organization require significant amounts of work with people outside my own group or department.

☐ The ability to build trust across departments is a valued quality in this organization.

☐ The ability to create a climate of openness and candor is highly prized in this organization.

☐ People feel that they're contributing most to this organization when they're helping all groups, not just their own, be successful.

☐ People in this organization operate under the philosophy that it's better to let everyone learn from your experience, even your mistakes.

What are the implications of your organization's culture for you as a leader? Do you see a good match between the culture and how you prefer to lead?

_____

_____

_____

_____

_____

4. Of the nine common views, perspectives, or philosophies on leadership that follow, which ones most closely reflect your own? Which most closely reflect the view of your organization?

1 = Does not reflect   2 = Slightly reflects   3 = Moderately reflects   4 = Closely reflects
5 = Definitely reflects

	My view as a leader	My organization's view
Leaders are born. Some people have leadership talent, and others do not.		
Leadership can be learned. With enough study and practice, anyone can become a more effective leader.		
Leaders are heroes. Charismatic and attractive, they perform feats that are beyond the abilities of ordinary people.		
Leaders are at the top. People follow their orders because they hold senior positions in the organization.		
Leaders are called to serve. When it's their time to lead, people will be asked.		
Leaders are defined by position. The leader's power and authority come with the job and the title.		
Leaders depend on and are created by others. A leader's goal is to enable the talents of other people.		
Leadership is temporary. When no leaders are available, people take on interim leadership roles.		
Leaders are servants. People lead for personal reasons: a deep sense of mission, purpose, inevitability, or legacy.		

On which perspectives is your own view closest to that of your organization? On which is it the furthest apart? What are the implications of your responses for your journey as a leader?

Closest:

_____

Furthest apart:

_____

Implications:

_____

_____

_____

5. What are your rules and norms at work? Which ones are shared by your organization? Check those norms that apply. Add any that are not listed.

Rule or norm	Mine at work	Shared by my organization
Recognize others.		
Take responsibility for my actions.		
Share the credit.		
Respect others' points of view even if I disagree.		
Come early and stay late.		
Speak up when I see a problem.		
Ignore problems.		

(continued)

Rule or norm	Mine at work	Shared by my organization
Help others.		
Challenge others.		
Welcome challenges and take risks.		
Share knowledge.		
The customer comes first.		
Build strong relationships.		
Protect your people and your function.		
Hire the best people.		
Develop talent from within.		
Give direct feedback on performance.		
Other:		

Are most of your important rules and norms also an integral part of your organization's culture?

_____Yes   _____No   _____Not sure

What are the implications of your answer to the above question for your journey as a leader?

_____

_____

_____

_____

_____

Think about the rules or norms you live by outside work. To what extent is there overlap between work and nonwork norms? Briefly describe the similarities and differences.

_____

_____

_____

_____

_____

6. When people aspire to positions of leadership, they often think of the benefits, without always considering that leadership also has its costs. Imagine that you are about to coach someone who has expressed interest in becoming a leader. Think back over all your experiences as a leader, including those in your current role. What have been some of your most difficult experiences as a leader? Why were they difficult?

_____

_____

_____

_____

_____

Following is a list of costs that leaders frequently mention—although what one leader considers a cost, another might consider a benefit of leadership. Based on your experiences, which items on this list do you consider as costs to you for being a leader? Which, if any, would you consider a benefit of leadership? Put check marks in the appropriate columns.

	Cost	Benefit
Increased visibility		
Required public duties		
Loss of peer relationships with colleagues		
Responsibility for direct reports' careers		
Increased demands requiring more stamina		
Increased job insecurity		
Need to watch what I say and how I behave		
Less time to spend with family		
Less honest feedback from others		
Other (specify):		
Other (specify):		
Other (specify):		

Briefly describe the implications of your responses to you as a leader:

_____

_____

_____

7. An important trend that affects leaders is the growing diversification of the workforce. Use the following activity, adapted from *Developing Cultural Adaptability: How to Work Across Differences* (Deal & Prince, 2003), to determine whether you have the attitudes and behaviors that are important for working with people from other cultures.

Rate yourself on each statement using this key:

5	One of my greatest strengths
4	Something I am good at
3	Something I can do but I need to improve a little
2	Something I can do but I need to improve a lot
1	Something I am not able to do
0	Don't know

I can operate effectively in a foreign language, even if through translation. _____

I am sensitive to differences between cultures. _____

I work hard to understand the perspectives of people from other cultures when we are working together. _____

I like to experience different cultures. _____

I am quick to change my behavior to match a new environment (for example, when assigned to a foreign country). _____

I enjoy the challenge of working in countries other than my own. _____

I understand how culture influences the way people express disagreement. _____

I can use cultural differences as a source of strength for the organization. _____

I am aware of my own deeply held beliefs when dealing with others. _____

I know when to hold fast to personal values and when to consider others' values. _____

I effectively surface my own and others' deeply held assumptions, values, or beliefs before making important decisions. _____

I can manage culture shock. _____

I can adapt my management style to meet cultural expectations. _____

Total score: _____

Worksheet scoring
Total score

32–42	Novice: I have limited experience working across cultures and am not particularly aware of the ways this influences my interactions.
43–52	Intermediate: With conscious effort, I can anticipate cultural differences, see others' perspectives, and change the way I interact with them.
53–64	Expert: I am able to easily work across cultures, perhaps in multiple languages. I am knowledgeable about many cultures, and can adopt an appropriate style for most interactions.

EXPAND YOUR LEARNING

The activities that follow can help you learn more about organizational realities, demands, and expectations and the ways in which they affect you as a leader. Note your observations and responses to questions in your leadership journal:

1. Find the names of five top futurists, study what they have to say, and identify several future trends and describe the ways that they might have an impact on your organization and your role as a leader in that organization. One place to start looking is the Web site for the Institute for the Future.

2. Metaphors are an excellent way to help you think about different types of leadership. The CCL Leadership Metaphor Explorer tool can be used to explore the types of leadership in your organization, the types of leaders you most want to emulate, and the types of leaders with whom you work at your best. For more information about the tool, including how to obtain it, visit www.ccl.org and type "Leadership Metaphor Explorer" in the search box on the home page.

THEMES AND PATTERNS

Use the following questions and activities to pull together what you have learned in this chapter about trends, leadership perspectives, and costs:

1. Having done the activities in this chapter, how clear would you say you are about the context in which you lead, your new perspective or philosophy of leadership, and the costs of leading?

The context in which I lead: _____Very clear   _____Somewhat clear   _____Not very clear

My philosophy of leadership: _____Very clear   _____Somewhat clear   _____Not very clear

The costs of leading: _____Very clear   _____Somewhat clear   _____Not very clear

If you answered "not very clear" to any of these questions, you might want to continue exploring the topic by consulting some of the resources listed at the end of the book.

2. As we noted in Chapter One, Ernest Hemingway was once challenged in a bar to write a very short story. He wrote the following six words: "For sale. Baby shoes. Never worn."

Try it yourself. Reflect on your responses to the questions in this chapter. Then write a six-word story that expresses what you have learned in this chapter about organizational realities, demands, and expectations. (As an alternative, write six words that summarize the major takeaway points or learning from the chapter.)

_____ _____ _____ _____ _____ _____

3. What other insights have you had from this chapter?

_____

_____

_____

_____

4. Write a one- to two-paragraph letter to yourself about the ways in which organizational realities, demands, and expectations are important to your role as a leader. Address the following:

- What impact do organizational realities have on you as a leader?

- What costs or demands are shaping your current feelings about being a leader?

- Based on what you have discovered in this chapter, what changes might you want or need to make in the way you approach your leadership role?

LETTER TO MYSELF

_____

_____

_____

_____

_____

_____

_____

_____

_____

_____

NOW WHAT?

What will you do to use what you have learned in this chapter? Which actions can you take immediately? Which actions require the help of others? Whose help do you need? What can you do to get it?

Action	Can take now? Yes or No?	Requires help from	To get help, I will

Write down what you still need to explore and understand about the impact of organizational realities, demands, and expectations on you as a leader:

_____

_____

_____

_____

_____

WHAT'S NEXT?

In Chapter Three, you will learn how a clear, compelling leadership vision that is connected to your personal vision can clarify your actions and choices and help lead you out of drift.

CHAPTER THREE

YOUR LEADERSHIP VISION

A vision that describes the future you want for yourself and your team, organization, or community provides the foundation for your leadership. Your leadership vision is different from the organizational mission that describes the reason your organization exists; instead, it expresses what you personally want to create, do, and accomplish as a leader. A component of your personal vision, your leadership vision can help you accomplish the larger vision for your life. The ability to articulate a compelling and easily understood leadership vision can help you chart a course out of drift.

To be useful in guiding you toward where you want to go, your leadership vision should incorporate your dreams and passions, be authentic and reflect your values, and continue to evolve as you proceed on your own life journey.

WHAT'S IN THIS CHAPTER?

The questions and activities in this chapter will help you:

- Understand the ways in which your leadership vision is foundational to your ability to be a successful leader
- Develop and articulate a leadership vision that is connected to your personal vision, is an authentic representation of who you are as a leader, and is clear and compelling to yourself and to others
- Make more conscious choices to align your vision and the work you do

LEARNING OBJECTIVES

When you complete this chapter, you will be able to:
- Articulate a leadership vision that is closely connected to your personal vision and your purpose for wanting to be a leader
- Make more conscious choices to align your vision and the work you do

YOUR CURRENT STATE

Answer the questions that follow to see how well you understand your current personal and leadership visions and the connections between them.

1. Do you currently have a personal vision that describes what you want to accomplish in your life? A leadership vision that expresses what you want to accomplish with your leadership? In the left-hand column that follows, list ten words or short phrases that express the essence of your personal vision. In the right-hand column, write ten words or short phrases that express the essence of your leadership vision.

My personal vision   ***My leadership vision***

_____   _____

_____   _____

_____   _____

_____   _____

_____   _____

_____   _____

_____   _____

_____   _____

What connections do you see between your personal vision and your leadership vision? Draw solid lines to connect any elements that are directly connected and dotted lines to connect any elements that are indirectly connected.

What, if any, conflicts do you see between your personal vision and your leadership vision? For example, might seeking a higher-level executive position conflict with your desire to spend more time with your family or volunteering in your community?

_____

_____

_____

_____

_____

2. Can you think of an event, experience, or series of events and experiences that would illustrate your personal vision? Your leadership vision? Write the key points of your personal experiences below:

Personal vision:

_____

_____

_____

_____

_____

Leadership vision:

_____

_____

_____

_____

_____

EXPLORE THE TOPIC

In this section, you will assess and discover or clarify a meaningful leadership vision that will be clear and compelling and provide guidance when you find yourself in a state of drift.

1. Think of a person who has a leadership vision that resonates with you. This can be someone you have read or heard about or someone you know well.

Write ten words that seem to convey the essence of this person's leadership vision:

_____ _____

_____ _____

_____ _____

_____ _____

_____ _____

What makes this leader's vision compelling?

_____

_____

_____

_____

_____

What are some actions this leader takes to communicate his or her vision?

_____

_____

_____

_____

What do you know about this person's personal vision—what he or she hopes to accomplish in life? In what ways do the person's personal vision and leadership vision appear to intersect?

_____

_____

_____

_____

_____

In what ways does this person's clear and compelling leadership vision affect his or her effectiveness as a leader?

_____

_____

_____

_____

_____

2. Think about another person you admire. This time, select someone who has been or is a role model or mentor to you. Write a few words that describe what you admire about this person, including any connections you see between this person's personal vision and his or her leadership vision.

_____

_____

_____

_____

_____

Now think about people you mentor or to whom you serve as a role model. Do you ever have conversations with them about vision (directly or indirectly)? If so, write a few words that describe the topics you have talked about or the advice you have given them.

_____

_____

_____

_____

_____

3. Write the essentials of a story that you could tell to convey to others how you became a leader or the reasons that you want to be a leader. Make your story brief, specific, and personal.

_____

_____

_____

_____

_____

4. Daydreams can be important sources of insight that connect present realities to a desired future state. Without overthinking this exercise, write ten words or phrases that describe the themes of your most common daydreams.

_____   _____

_____   _____

_____   _____

_____   _____

_____   _____

Look at what you wrote. What insights do you draw from the themes?

_____

_____

_____

_____

_____

Now imagine that you are daydreaming about being an exceptional leader. Without stopping to think, write ten words that describe your behavior as an exceptional leader.

_____   _____

_____   _____

_____   _____

_____   _____

_____   _____

What themes do you see? What are the gaps between your current leadership behavior and how you envision yourself as an exceptional leader?

Themes:

_____

_____

_____

_____

_____

Gaps:

_____

_____

_____

_____

_____

5. Achieving your leadership vision often entails using power and influence. In doing so, you are likely to encounter some interpersonal conflict. Do the following to articulate your thoughts and feelings about power and conflict.

a. Set a timer for one minute. Then without stopping to think, write every word and phrase in the Power and Conflict box that comes to mind when you think of these terms.

POWER AND CONFLICT

_____

_____

_____

_____

_____

_____

_____

_____

_____

b. Reflect on the words and phrases that you wrote. Then read the following statements and check any that seem to apply to you.

☐ I am comfortable with having power.

☐ I try to avoid using power.

☐ I seldom misuse power.

☐ I often use my power to get what I want.

☐ I know how to collaborate with others in positions of power to accomplish a vision.

☐ I am comfortable with conflict.

☐ I am skilled at dealing with conflict.

☐ I try to avoid conflict.

☐ I will fight for what I think is right.

Did any of your responses surprise you? If so, what are the implications for you as a leader?

_____

_____

_____

_____

_____

6. Imagine that a journalist is going to interview you about your leadership vision. Write ten words or phrases that capture the essence of that vision.

_____   _____

_____   _____

_____   _____

_____   _____

_____   _____

7. What personal, environmental, or organizational factors currently present obstacles to enacting your leadership vision? What actions could you take to eliminate or remove those obstacles?

Obstacle	*Actions for eliminating or removing*
_____	_____
_____	_____
_____	_____
_____	_____
_____	_____

EXPAND YOUR LEARNING

The next activities can help you learn more about leadership visions so you can clarify your own. Note your observations and responses to questions in your leadership journal.

1. Look for examples of leadership visions. You can find them by interviewing people about their visions; searching for documents (such as annual reports, company Web sites, letters to donors, magazines, and taglines on e-mails) in which people have articulated their visions; and looking through biographies and autobiographies. Make notes of the key concepts and statements you find. Then compare the different leadership visions that you find and consider these questions:

   - What's similar? What's different? What connections do you see between what you found and your own vision for leadership?

   - What is the connection (or lack thereof) between the visions that people articulate and what actually happens in practice?

   - What have you learned that you can use to develop or revise your own leadership vision?

2. Take a blank sheet of paper and some colored pens or a whiteboard with colored markers to a quiet, private place and do the following:

   - Put on some music that you enjoy. Close your eyes and listen quietly for a few minutes.

   - Open your eyes and, without stopping to think, draw whatever images come to mind when you think about your vision for leadership. It doesn't matter if you can't draw well. Just let the pens move over the paper or whiteboard and see what comes out.

   - Turn off the music. Step back and look at what you have drawn. In your leadership journal, describe what you see in the drawing that relates to your leadership vision.

3. Ask several people who know you well—friends, family, colleagues—to describe their understanding of your leadership vision. Compare their perceptions with your own. What similarities are there? What differences? What are the implications for you as a leader?

4. Use the following activity, adapted from *Creating a Vision* (Criswell & Cartwright, 2010), to stimulate your thinking and help clarify your leadership vision.

   - Gather at least twenty images from magazines, postcards, photographs, or online resources. Look for images that you find interesting or compelling in some way, without stopping to analyze your reasons for your selections.

   - Sit quietly for a few moments and focus on this question: "How will the world look different as a result of my work as a leader?"

   - Look through the images you have collected, and identify the one that most closely represents your answer to that question.

5. Write down your thoughts about this image and how it relates to leadership. Use these questions as prompts to guide you:

   - Describe the image. What do you actually see? What colors, shapes, and details are in your picture? What stands out?

   - Why did you select it?

   - How does it relate to leadership?

   - What inspires you about the picture?

- How does the picture relate to your challenges?
- What does it say about where you've been?
- What does it say about where you are today?
- What does it say about where you are going?
- How do you connect your image with the thoughts and themes that emerged from your initial vision journal writing?
- Do you now have any fresh perspectives or new insights relating to your organization's vision?

THEMES AND PATTERNS

Pull together what you have learned in this chapter about leadership vision:

1. Having done the activities in this chapter, how clear would you say you were about your vision of leadership and its connection to your personal vision?

My vision of leadership: _____Very clear   _____Somewhat clear   _____Not very clear

Connection between my
leadership vision and
my personal vision: _____Very clear   _____Somewhat clear   _____Not very clear

If you answered "not very clear" to either of these questions, you might want to continue exploring the topic by consulting some of the resources listed at the end of the book.

2. Reflect on your responses to the questions in this chapter. Then write a six-word story that expresses what you have learned about your leadership vision and its connection to your personal vision. (As an alternative, write six words that summarize the major takeaway points or learning from the chapter.)

_____ _____ _____ _____ _____ _____

What other insights did you take from this chapter?

_____

_____

_____

_____

_____

3. Write a one- to two-paragraph letter to yourself that articulates your leadership vision and describes what you can do to communicate that vision to others.

LETTER TO MYSELF

_____

_____

_____

_____

_____

_____

_____

_____

_____

NOW WHAT?

What will you do to use what you have learned in this chapter? Which actions can you take immediately? Which actions require the help of others? Whose help do you need? What can you do to get it?

Action	Can take now? Yes or No?	Requires help from	To get help, I will

What do you still need to explore and understand about how to articulate and communicate your leadership vision?

_____

_____

_____

_____

_____

WHAT'S NEXT?

In addition to having a clear, compelling leadership vision, having insight into the motivations and core values that drive your leadership can help you avoid or chart a course out of drift. You'll learn about motivations and values in the next chapter.

CHAPTER FOUR

YOUR LEADERSHIP MOTIVATIONS AND VALUES

Awareness of your motivations and values helps you understand why you are or want to be a leader and what kind of leader you want to be; determine what to do when conflicts occur; and make important choices and decisions about your leadership. When you experience drift, being aware of your motivations and values can also help you understand your leadership.

Motivations are powerful forces that compel you to action. The sources of motivation are different for each person but they generally include validation, rewards, impact, service, and meaning.

Values such as achievement, challenge, friendship, justice, loyalty, recognition, and status are the standards or principles that guide your beliefs, decisions, and actions. Your core values drive your life decisions, bear on the way you set priorities, direct your leadership vision, and guide your leadership choices. Core values come from and are influenced by many factors, including culture, personal history, social milieu, mentors, vocation, and organization.

The congruence between your core values (what you believe is important) and your actions (what you say and do) is often called authenticity; it is a critical leadership quality that makes others want to follow and helps you help others lead. Conflicts between your core values and that of your organization can contribute to drift.

WHAT'S IN THIS CHAPTER?

The questions and activities in this chapter will help you:
- Learn more about why you want to lead (or clarify why you have found yourself in a leadership role) and why you are attracted to certain leadership roles and opportunities
- Assess what motivates you the most, identify your core values, and make more conscious choices to align your motivations and values with the work you do
- Determine whether your current role or organization is a good fit for you
- Gain more insight into the foundation of your excitement, optimism, passion, and enthusiasm so that you can be more successful at leading others and encouraging them to be part of your vision
- Clarify the connection between your leadership vision and your core values

LEARNING OBJECTIVES

When you complete this chapter, you will be able to:
- Describe your own motivators for leading
- List in order of importance the eight to twelve core values that guide your beliefs, decisions, and actions
- Describe actions you can take to better align your motivations and values with the work you do

YOUR CURRENT STATE

These questions will help you assess what you already know about your motivations and values.

1. Reflect on your experiences in school and at work. Then briefly answer the questions that follow.

- Which projects or types of projects did you enjoy the most? Why? What elements were present—for example, fun people to work with, learning something new, high visibility, or solving a critical problem?

_____

_____

_____

_____

_____

- Which projects or types of projects did you enjoy the least? Why?

_____

_____

_____

_____

_____

2. Think about the aspects of your work that energize you and those that zap your energy. List some of them below:

Aspects of my work that energize me	*Aspects of my work that drain my energy*
_____	_____
_____	_____
_____	_____
_____	_____
_____	_____

3. In Chapter One, we described flow as times when you are so absorbed in an activity that you lose your sense of time and place. Briefly describe what you were doing the last time you felt that you were in the flow at work.

_____

_____

_____

_____

_____

How often in the past month have you felt that way?

_____

4. Without stopping to think, write a few words and phrases below that describe what excites and interests you about leading.

_____

_____

_____

_____

_____

5. Have you ever chosen to leave a position because the job or the organization didn't feel as if it was the right fit for you? Briefly describe the job and your reasons for leaving.

_____

_____

_____

6. How well do you know what values drive your behavior, both at work and outside work? Without stopping to think, list your top ten values in each category.

	Values at work	*Values outside work*
1.		
2.		
3.		
4.		
5.		
6.		
7.		
8.		
9.		
10.		

EXPLORE THE TOPIC

The questions in this section are intended to help you examine your motivations and values in more depth and identify possible conflicts between your values and those of your organization.

1. What motivates you to be a leader? Think about how important each of the motivators is to you, and circle the number that best describes this. (At the bottom of the list, you can add others that are important to you.)

1 = Not important   2 = Not very important   3 = Neither important nor unimportant
4 = Somewhat important   5 = Very important

Validation—the affirmations you receive from others	1	2	3	4	5
Rewards—prestige, status, respect, inclusion, recognition, money, other nonmonetary rewards	1	2	3	4	5
Impact—the urge to make a difference, to see the results of your efforts	1	2	3	4	5
Service—to help others and make the world a better place	1	2	3	4	5
Meaning—to find greater clarity about how to craft a meaningful life	1	2	3	4	5
Other motivators:					
	1	2	3	4	5
	1	2	3	4	5
	1	2	3	4	5

For the motivators that you rated a 4 or 5, how well are they being met in your current role?

Motivator: _____

_____Not being met   _____Being met to some degree   _____Being met

Motivator: _____

_____Not being met   _____Being met to some degree   _____Being met

Motivator: _____

_____Not being met   _____Being met to some degree   _____Being met

What do your ratings tell you about the factors that drive you? How consistent is your current leadership role with your most important motivators?

_____

_____

_____

_____

_____

2. If someone were to assess your leadership based on your behavior—what you say and do—what might the person assume motivates you?

_____

_____

_____

_____

_____

3. Think of a particular role model or mentor in your life (this can be the same person you thought about in Chapter Three). Describe the values you think this person holds, based on his or her behavior.

_____

_____

_____

_____

_____

4. Use the following activity, adapted from *Setting Priorities: Personal Values, Organizational Results* (Cartwright, 2007), to help you identify your motivators and values. Think about two or three people with whom you enjoy working or with whom you would like to work, and two or three people with whom you do not enjoy working or with whom you would prefer not to work. Write a few words to describe the characteristics that you appreciate and admire or do not appreciate and admire about each of those people:

Name	Enjoy working with or would like to work with	Do not enjoy working with or would prefer not to work with
_____	_____	_____
_____	_____	_____
_____	_____	_____
_____	_____	_____
_____	_____	_____
_____	_____	_____
_____	_____	_____

What do the characteristics you identified tell you about what you consider to be your important motivators and values?

_____

_____

_____

_____

_____

5. Look at the values listed in the Common Values chart shown here. Take some time to reflect on what's important to you. Then rate each value according to its importance to you.

Common Values

Rate each value in this list according to how important the value is to you, using the following scale. Add any important values that are not listed.

1 = Always valued   2 = Often valued   3 = Sometimes valued   4 = Seldom valued   5 = Never valued

_____ Achievement—a sense of accomplishment, mastery, goal achievement

_____ Activity—fast-paced, highly active work

_____ Advancement—growth, seniority, and promotion resulting from work well done

_____ Adventure—new and challenging opportunities, excitement, risk

_____ Aesthetics—appreciation of beauty in things, ideas, surroundings, personal space

_____ Affiliation—interaction with other people, recognition as a member of a particular group, involvement, belonging

_____ Affluence—high income, financial success, prosperity

_____ Authority—position and power to control events and other people's activities

_____ Autonomy—ability to act independently with few constraints, self-sufficiency, self-reliance, ability to make most decisions and choices

_____ Balance—lifestyle that allows for time for self, family, work, and community

_____ Challenge—continually facing complex and demanding tasks and problems

_____ Change and variation—absence of routine; work responsibilities, daily activities, or settings that change frequently; unpredictability

_____ Collaboration—close, cooperative working relationships with groups

_____ Community—serving and supporting a purpose that supersedes personal desires; making a difference

_____ Competency—demonstrating high proficiency and knowledge, showing above-average effectiveness and efficiency at tasks

_____ Competition—rivalry with winning as the goal

_____ Courage—willingness to stand up for one's beliefs

_____ Creativity—discovering, developing, or designing new ideas, formats, programs, or things; demonstrating innovation and imagination

_____ Diverse perspectives—unusual ideas and opinions, points of view that may not seem right or be popular at first but bear fruit in the long run

(continued)

_____ Duty—respect for authority, rules, and regulations

_____ Economic security—steady and secure employment, adequate financial reward, low risk

_____ Enjoyment—fun, joy, and laughter

_____ Fame—prominence, being well known

_____ Family—spending time with partner, children, parents, or extended family

_____ Friendship—close personal relationships with others

_____ Health—physical and mental well-being, vitality

_____ Helping others—helping people attain their goals, providing care and support

_____ Humor—the ability to laugh at oneself and life

_____ Influence—having an impact or effect on the attitudes or opinions of other people, persuasiveness

_____ Inner harmony—happiness, contentment, being at peace with oneself

_____ Integrity—acting in accordance with moral and ethical standards; honesty, sincerity, truth; trustworthiness

_____ Justice—fairness, equality, doing the right thing

_____ Knowledge—the pursuit of understanding, skill, and expertise; continuous learning

_____ Location—choice of a place to live that is conducive to one's lifestyle

_____ Love—involvement in close, affectionate relationships; intimacy

_____ Loyalty—faithfulness; dedication to individuals, traditions, or organizations

_____ Order—stability, routine, predictability, clear lines of authority, standardized procedures

_____ Personal development—dedication to maximizing one's potential

_____ Physical fitness—staying in shape through exercise and physical activity

_____ Recognition—positive feedback and public credit for work well done; respect and admiration

_____ Responsibility—dependability, reliability, accountability for results

_____ Self-respect—pride, self-esteem, sense of personal identity

_____ Spirituality—strong spiritual or religious beliefs, moral fulfillment

_____ Status—being respected for one's job or one's association with a prestigious group or organization

_____ Wisdom—sound judgment based on knowledge, experience, and understanding

Now take a close look at the values that you rated Always Valued or Often Valued. Ask yourself these questions about each of them, and decide whether you wish to change the rating:

- Is this value important to me now, or is it a value that was important to me in the past?

- Have I included this value because it really has meaning for me, or because it is socially or politically correct?

- Have I included this value because someone else might have done so, even though it does not have a significant meaning for me?

- How did I determine that this value is something that I always value instead of often value, or vice versa?

- Would other people observing my behavior agree that this value is an important one for me?

Finally, look again at the values that you would still rate Always Valued. Choose *no more* than fifteen of those values—the ones most important to you—and write them on the lines below. These are your core values—the ones that profoundly affect who you are as a person and a leader.

My core values

_____   _____

_____   _____

_____   _____

_____   _____

_____   _____

_____   _____

_____

What, if any, potential conflicts do you see between one core value and another (for example, creativity versus order, competition versus collaboration). Describe those conflicts below:

_____

_____

_____

_____

_____

How well do you think that your leadership behaviors and choices are aligned with your core values?

_____Very well _____Reasonably well _____Not very well _____ Not well at all

If you selected "not very well" or "not well at all," what do you think are some reasons?

_____

_____

_____

_____

_____

How well does your current leadership role support or fulfill your core values?

_____Very well _____Reasonably well _____Not very well _____Not well at all

What actions can you take to create a stronger connection of your values with your leadership role?

_____

_____

_____

_____

_____

6. Values are reflected in an organization's behavior as well as in its policies and formal practices—for example, how it treats its employees, stakeholders, and customers; how it handles conflict and change; and how it encourages innovation and entrepreneurs. In some organizations, there may be a difference between the organization's written values and the values expressed through people's behavior.

Reflect on the types of leadership that are exhibited and rewarded in your organization. (If you did the Leadership Metaphor Explorer exercise in Chapter Two, take another look at it.)

- Based on the behaviors that you observe in your organization, what values does your organization support? What values are rewarded?

_____

_____

_____

_____

_____

- Think about the organization's top leaders. Based on their words and actions, which values appear to be most prominent?

_____

_____

_____

_____

_____

- What are the organization's stated or written values?

_____

_____

_____

_____

_____

- Do you see any disconnect or conflict between the stated or written values, the behaviors the organization rewards, and the actions that senior leaders take? If yes, describe the disconnects, and explain possible reasons for them.

_____

_____

_____

_____

_____

- How well do your values fit with the organization's view of leadership? Are they in conflict? If so, in what ways? What are the implications for you?

_____

_____

_____

_____

_____

- How well do the organizational values match your own core values? Do you see any conflict between your values and those of the organization? If so, what is the conflict?

_____

_____

_____

_____

_____

- Think about your personal and leadership visions—what you want to accomplish in your life and what you want to accomplish as a leader. What values are represented? Are any of your core values missing? Which ones? What, if any, conflicts do you see between your core values and your visions, and what will you do to reconcile the differences?

_____

_____

_____

_____

EXPAND YOUR LEARNING

Do the activities below to deepen your understanding of the motivations and values that shape your leadership. Note your observations and responses to the questions in your leadership journal.

1. Watch a movie, read a book, or search the Internet with the goal of identifying two or three people who have exhibited outstanding leadership. What did they do or say that you consider outstanding? What values and motivations might be behind their words and actions?

2. Ask several people who know you well—friends, family members, colleagues, managers—what they think motivates you to be a leader and what values your leadership behaviors exhibit. Compare what they say to your own understanding of your motivations and values.

3. To get a better idea of how your values motivate you to set priorities, track all your activities for a typical week. Include personal activities and work activities.

4. When the week is over, look for the relationships between your values and how you actually spend your time. For example, if family is one of your core values, how much time did you spend with your family? If advancement or promotion is a core value, how much time did you devote to activities that would help you move forward in your career? Think about whether you would like to make any changes in the ways in which you spend your time so that your actions are more congruent with the values that motivate you and what it would take to make those changes.

THEMES AND PATTERNS

Answer the questions below to consolidate what you learned in the chapter about your leadership motivations and values.

1. Having done the activities in this chapter, how clear would you say you were about your leadership motivations and values?

My leadership motivations: ____Very clear   ____Somewhat clear   ____Not very clear

My values: ____Very clear   ____Somewhat clear   ____Not very clear

The connections between my values and my motivations:

____Very clear ____Somewhat clear ____Not very clear

The fit between my core values and those of my organization:

____Very good fit ____Okay fit ____Not a good fit

The extent to which my core values are represented in my personal and leadership visions:

____Well represented ____Somewhat represented ____Not well represented

If you answered "not very clear," "not a good fit," or "not well represented" to any of these questions, you might want to continue exploring the topic by consulting some of the resources listed at the end of the book.

2. Reflect on your responses to the questions in this chapter. Then write a six-word story that expresses what you have learned in this chapter about your motivations and values. (As an alternative, write six words that summarize the major takeaway points or learning from the chapter.)

_____ _____ _____ _____ _____ _____

3. What other insights have you had from this chapter?

_____

_____

_____

4. Write a one- to two-paragraph letter to yourself about what motivates you to lead and the values that guide your beliefs, decisions, and actions.

- What relationship do you see between what motivates you to lead and your core values?
- How are your core values reflected in your leadership behaviors?
- How are your motivations and values connected to your leadership vision?

LETTER TO MYSELF

_____

_____

_____

_____

_____

_____

_____

_____

_____

_____

_____

_____

_____

_____

_____

_____

_____

NOW WHAT?

What will you do to use what you have learned in this chapter? Which actions can you take immediately? Which actions require the help of others? Whose help do you need? What can you do to get it?

Action	Can take now? Yes or No?	Requires help from	To get help, I will

What do you still need to explore and understand about your leadership motivations and values and their connection to any feelings you have about being stuck or drifting?

_____

_____

_____

_____

_____

WHAT'S NEXT?

Now that you have a good understanding of the motivations and values that drive your leadership, you will next examine your leadership profile: the personal styles, competencies, responses to change, and work experiences that are important to your leadership and the leadership choices that you make.

CHAPTER FIVE

YOUR LEADERSHIP PROFILE

Your leadership profile defines who you are as a leader and what you bring to your leadership roles. The better you understand your profile, the better able you will be to become more agile and flexible, gain more insight into how your behaviors affect others, recognize diversity in others' needs, and learn from your experiences.

Understanding your leadership profile means assessing yourself on eleven foundational leadership competencies (the skills and abilities you need to be a leader); the roles you play, either formally or informally, as a leader; the learning tactics you prefer; your change style (how you respond to change); the life and career experiences that have provided you with information, wisdom, and expertise; and derailment factors (the behaviors or gaps that can cause you to lose your way and block your success as a leader).

WHAT'S IN THIS CHAPTER?

The questions and activities in this chapter will help you:

- Understand the essential elements of a leadership profile
- Discover and examine your own leadership profile so you can determine how best to leverage profile components across situations and people to improve your effectiveness and prevent derailment

LEARNING OBJECTIVES

When you complete this chapter, you will be able to:
- Assess yourself on each of the six essential elements of a leadership profile
- Explain how each element of your profile contributes to your current state of drift or of being "in the zone"
- Identify steps you can take to avoid the five factors that can lead to derailment
- Connect your leadership profile to your leadership vision and values

YOUR CURRENT STATE

These questions will help you assess what you already know about the elements of your leadership profile:

1. If you were leading in a completely authentic way (that is, consistent with your values, vision, and leadership philosophy), what would your leadership behaviors look like? Don't overthink this question; just take two minutes to write down everything that comes to mind in the Authentic Leadership box.

After you have finished, think next about a time when you were *not* leading in a way that was authentic to your true self. Take another two minutes to write down the behaviors you were engaging in that were inconsistent with your authentic self. Again, don't overthink this question; just write down everything that comes to mind in the Inauthentic Leadership box on page 70.

AUTHENTIC LEADERSHIP

Inauthentic Leadership

_____

_____

_____

_____

_____

_____

_____

_____

_____

_____

_____

_____

_____

_____

_____

_____

_____

_____

_____

_____

2. If a neutral observer were to ask your boss (or your most recent boss) to name your top three to five strengths and your top three to five areas for improvement, what do you think he or she would mention?

Strengths   *Areas for improvement*

_____   _____

_____   _____

_____   _____

_____   _____

_____   _____

To what extent would you agree or disagree with your boss's assessment? Briefly explain your reasons.

_____

_____

_____

_____

_____

3. How do you typically respond to change? Reflect on two or three recent changes at work or in your personal life. How did you feel about the change? How did you respond? What did you do to make the necessary adaptations and adjustments?

_____

_____

_____

4. Think about experiences, assignments, and challenges that you have had in your current job or in previous jobs that have had a lasting impact on you as a

leader. Briefly describe two or three of them. For each one, write a few words that explain the most important things you learned from these experiences.

_____

_____

_____

EXPLORE THE TOPIC

Use the following questions to examine your leadership profile so you can identify your strengths and your developmental priorities—your areas for improvement.

1. The eleven leadership competencies in the chart here are critical for today's leaders. Circle the appropriate letter to the left of each competency to indicate whether that competency is a strength for you, important to your current leadership role, or something that will become important for you as a leader in the future. At the bottom of the chart, add any other competencies that are critical to your current or future role as a leader.

Use the space next to each competency to add notes about what you might do to develop competencies that are not currently strengths but that might become more important in the future.

S = Currently a strength for me

C = Important to my current role as a leader

F = Important for my future role as a leader

S C F	Demonstrating integrity
S C F	Building trust

S C F	Getting things done through others
S C F	Developing others
S C F	Communicating well
S C F	Building teams
S C F	Technological savvy
S C F	Comfort with ambiguity and uncertainty
S C F	Flexibility and adaptability
S C F	Creating networks and alliances

S C F	Global astuteness
S C F	Other (specify):
S C F	Other (specify):
S C F	Other (specify):

2. Every leader plays a variety of roles. Many common roles are shown below. Circle the roles that are most frequently valued and rewarded in your organization.

Advocate	Facilitator	Mediator	Organizer
Astute observer	Fixer	Mentor	People developer
Change agent	Implementer	Motivator	Problem solver
Coach	Innovator	Negotiator	Risk taker
Collaborator	Integrator	Networker	Strategist
Communicator	Learner	Nurturer	Team or community builder
Entrepreneur	Manager	Ombudsman	Visionary

Which roles do you most often play as a leader in your organization? List them on the following page, and indicate whether you are skilled or unskilled:

Role	*Skilled*	*Unskilled*
_____	_____	_____
_____	_____	_____
_____	_____	_____
_____	_____	_____
_____	_____	_____

Which other roles or functions listed above do you think will become more important as you move forward in your career? List them below. Then number them in order according to how important they will become to you as a leader in the future, and indicate whether you are skilled or unskilled at them.

Role	*Skilled*	*Unskilled*
_____	_____	_____
_____	_____	_____
_____	_____	_____
_____	_____	_____
_____	_____	_____

What concrete actions can you take to develop your ability to use the two or three roles that you indicated were the most important?

_____

_____

_____

_____

_____

3. Successful leaders are lifelong learners, and each individual has a preferred way of learning. Increasing your versatility as a learner begins with understanding the learning style you currently prefer. Use the following activity, adapted from *Becoming a More Versatile Learner* (Dalton, 1998), to help you identify your preferred learning style.

Following is a list of tactics representing four learning styles. Place a check mark in the box next to each statement that seems to be an accurate description of what you would do when faced with a challenging opportunity. Be as honest with yourself as you can.

Feeling tactics

When I am faced with a challenging opportunity:

- ☐ I carefully consider how I feel.
- ☐ I confront myself if I am avoiding the work challenge.
- ☐ I carefully consider how others might feel.
- ☐ I trust my feelings about what to do.
- ☐ I acknowledge the impact of my feelings on what I decide to do.

Action tactics

When I am faced with a challenging opportunity:

- ☐ I figure it out by trial and error.
- ☐ I allow my own experience to be my guide.
- ☐ I immerse myself in the situation to figure it out quickly.
- ☐ I don't allow lack of information or input to keep me from making my move.
- ☐ I commit myself to making something happen.

Thinking tactics

When I am faced with a challenging opportunity:

- ☐ I regularly access magazine articles, books, or the Internet to gain knowledge or information.
- ☐ I ask myself, "How is this similar to other things I know?"
- ☐ I imagine how different options might play out.
- ☐ I try to conceptualize the ideal response.
- ☐ I try to mentally rehearse my actions before entering the situation.

Accessing-others tactics

When I am faced with a challenging opportunity:

- ☐ I often seek the advice of those around me.

☐ I look for role models and try to emulate the behavior of these people.

☐ I find someone who can give me feedback about how I am doing.

☐ I look for a course or a training experience.

☐ I look for someone who has had experience in that area.

For which set of tactics did you mark the most statements? This is your primary learning style. Think about the learning styles you least prefer (the ones where you marked the fewest statements). What makes you less comfortable with those learning styles?

What insights have you gained from completing the learning styles inventory?

_____

_____

_____

_____

_____

What might you do to expand your ability to use different learning tactics?

_____

_____

_____

_____

_____

4. Leaders need to be able to respond effectively to change, but some are better at dealing with change than others. How well do you adjust and adapt to change? Use the following activity, adapted from *Adaptability: Responding Effectively to Change* (Calarco & Gurvis, 2006), to determine how well you adjust and adapt to change.

Think about some recent changes at work or in your personal life. Then rate the statements below on how well they describe you:

1 = Not at all   2 = To some degree   3 = Well   4 = Very well

_____ I accept change as positive.

_____ I see change as an opportunity.

_____ I adapt plans as necessary.

_____ I effectively involve others in the design and implementation of change.

_____ I quickly master new technology, vocabulary, and operating rules.

_____ I seek corrective feedback to improve.

_____ I sort out my strengths and weaknesses fairly accurately.

_____ I lead change by example.

_____ I take into account people's concerns during change.

_____ I effectively manage others' resistance to organizational changes.

_____ I relate to all kinds of individuals tactfully and fairly.

_____ I understand and respect cultural, religious, gender, and racial differences.

_____ I adjust my style to changing situations.

_____ I admit personal mistakes, learn from them, and move on.

_____ I value working with a diverse workforce.

_____ I am comfortable managing people different from myself.

_____ I am optimistic; I see the glass as half-full.

_____ I am not easily irritated when things are not going my way.

What do your ratings tell you about how well you adapt and adjust to change?

_____

_____

_____

_____

_____

What could you do to become more comfortable with change?

_____

_____

_____

_____

_____

5. Successful leaders continually learn from their experiences. What challenges at your current job or at previous jobs have broadened your experience and had a lasting effect on you as a leader? In the list of common job challenges that follows, check those that have been learning and developmental experiences for you. Briefly describe each challenge you checked and what you learned. Add any significant challenges that are not represented in this list.

☐ *Unfamiliar responsibilities*—handling responsibilities that are new or very different from previous ones you've handled

_____

_____

_____

_____

_____

☐ *New directions*—starting something new or making strategic changes

_____

_____

_____

_____

_____

☐ *Inherited problems*—fixing problems created by someone else or existing before you took the assignment

_____

_____

_____

_____

_____

☐ *Problems with employees*—dealing with employees who lack adequate experience, are incompetent, or are resistant to change

_____

_____

_____

_____

_____

☐ *High stakes*—managing work with tight deadlines, pressure from above, high visibility, and responsibility for critical decisions

_____

_____

_____

_____

_____

☐ *Scope and scale*—managing work that is broad in scope (involving multiple functions, groups, locations, products, or services) or large in sheer size (for example, workload, number of responsibilities)

_____

_____

_____

_____

_____

☐ *External pressure*—managing the interface with important groups outside the organization, such as customers, vendors, partners, unions, and regulatory agencies

_____

_____

_____

_____

☐ *Influence without authority*—influencing peers, higher management, or other key people over whom you have no authority

_____

_____

_____

_____

☐ *Work across cultures*—working with people from different cultures or with institutions in other countries

_____

_____

_____

_____

_____

☐ *Work for group diversity*—being responsible for the work of people of both genders and different racial and ethnic backgrounds

_____

_____

_____

_____

_____

☐ Other challenge (specify):

_____

_____

_____

_____

_____

☐ Other challenge (specify):

_____

_____

_____

_____

☐ Other challenge (specify):

_____

_____

_____

_____

What are some challenges you welcome as opportunities to develop yourself further?

_____

_____

_____

_____

6. Leaders who are well on their way to success—even those who have achieved a significant measure of success—can find their path forward blocked for a number of reasons. Take a careful and honest introspective look at yourself. Think about the formal and informal feedback you have received about your leadership and any previous or current problems you have had as a leader. What behaviors, even minor ones, might be consistent with factors that cause other leaders to derail? Check any of the factors in the list that follows that pose the risk of derailing you

in your quest to become a successful leader or continue on your career trajectory. For each factor you check, describe something you can do to reduce or eliminate the impediment. If you think of other factors that are not on the list, add them.

☐ *Problems with interpersonal relationships*
Action for reducing or eliminating: _____

_____

☐ *Difficulty leading a team*
Action for reducing or eliminating: _____

_____

☐ *Difficulty changing or adapting*
Action for reducing or eliminating: _____

_____

☐ *Failure to meet key organizational objectives*
Action for reducing or eliminating: _____

_____

☐ *A narrow functional orientation*
Action for reducing or eliminating: _____

_____

☐ Other (specify):

_____

Action for reducing or eliminating: _____

_____

☐ Other (specify):

_____

Action for reducing or eliminating: _____

_____

☐ Other (specify):

_____

Action for reducing or eliminating: _____

_____

7. What experiences, assignments, or learning opportunities would you like to have during the next five to ten years in order to be a more effective leader? Use the Desired Future Experiences chart to do the following:

a. In the left-hand column of the chart, list every experience, assignment, and learning opportunity that occurs to you, regardless of the cost, time commitment, or other practical consideration.

b. In the center column, briefly describe possible obstacles.

c. In the right-hand column, note possible ways to overcome the obstacles.

d. Number the items in order of priority to indicate which you think would have the highest impact on your continued development as a leader and which would have the lowest impact.

DESIRED FUTURE EXPERIENCES

Experiences, assignments, and learning opportunities	Possible obstacles	Actions for overcoming obstacles
_____	_____	_____
_____	_____	_____
_____	_____	_____
_____	_____	_____
_____	_____	_____
_____	_____	_____

(continued)

_____ _____ _____

_____ _____ _____

_____ _____ _____

_____ _____ _____

_____ _____ _____

_____ _____ _____

EXPAND YOUR LEARNING

The following activities can help you learn more about your leadership profile and the ways in which it influences your success as a leader. Note your observations and responses to the activities in your leadership journal.

1. Have you taken a 360-degree assessment in the past two or three years? If so, reexamine the results to identify the behaviors for which you have made progress and the areas on which you still need to work. If you have not taken a 360-degree assessment, consider doing so; it can provide valuable information about your strengths and weak areas as a leader.

2. Gain a deeper understanding of your competencies and skills by seeking feedback from your colleagues and your manager. Ask such questions as, "What do you consider my strengths as a leader? In what areas do you think I need to work? Is there anything that I can do personally to help you (or someone else) be more effective? Is there anything that I do now that interferes with your effectiveness or that is bothersome to you?"

THEMES AND PATTERNS

The following question and activities will help you pull together what you have learned in the chapter about your leadership profile:

1. Having completed the activities in this chapter, how clear are you on your leadership profile?

_____Very clear   _____Somewhat clear   _____Not very clear

If you answered "not very clear" to this question, you might want to continue exploring the topic by consulting some of the resources listed at the end of the book.

2. Reflect on your responses to the questions in this chapter. Then write a six-word story that expresses what you have learned in this chapter about when, where, and how you lead. (As an alternative, write six words that summarize the major takeaway points or learning from the chapter.)

_____ _____ _____ _____ _____ _____

3. Write a one- to two-paragraph letter to yourself that includes:

- The key elements of your leadership profile, including the strengths that make you a valued leader and the weaker areas on which you may need to work

- The connections between your leadership profile and your vision and core values

- Some steps you can take to continue to develop and reduce or avoid derailment

LETTER TO MYSELF

_____

_____

_____

_____

_____

_____

_____

_____

_____

_____

_____

_____

_____

_____

_____

NOW WHAT?

What will you do to use what you have learned in this chapter? Which actions can you take immediately? Which actions require the help of others? Whose help do you need? What can you do to get it?

Action	Can take now? Yes or No?	Requires help from	To get help, I will

What do you still need to explore and understand about the elements of your leadership profile and their connection to any feelings you have about being stuck or drifting?

_____

_____

_____

_____

_____

WHAT'S NEXT?

You have examined four of the five components of the Discovering Leadership Framework. In the next chapter, you will explore the fifth component: the personal realities, demands, and expectations that, with your work, provide the context that influences and shapes your leadership.

CHAPTER SIX

PERSONAL REALITIES, DEMANDS, AND EXPECTATIONS

Your life outside work surrounds and influences your work as a leader (and vice versa). Just as the organizational context creates certain demands and expectations, so does your personal context. Like most other leaders, you probably struggle with the tensions and interdependencies of your work and personal lives. While the lessons learned in your personal life can be helpful in your role as a leader, multiple conflicting priorities can lead to stress. Success as a leader means striving to achieve the right work-life balance for you.

WHAT'S IN THIS CHAPTER?

The questions and activities in this chapter will help you:

- Gain a better understanding of the interdependencies of your work and personal lives, including the benefits and costs
- Analyze the tensions between and impacts of the demands, expectations, and needs of your work situation and your life outside work, and determine the degree to which balance is an obtainable, even desirable, goal for you
- Decide how best to divide your focus, energy, and time across the multiple demands and expectations in order to be a more effective leader and develop strategies for achieving your optimum work-life balance

LEARNING OBJECTIVES

When you complete this chapter, you will be able to:
- Describe the benefits and costs of leading for both your work and personal lives
- Describe ways in which the lessons from your personal life can help you become a better leader and vice versa
- Identify strategies to help you achieve your definition of work-life balance

YOUR CURRENT STATE

The statements that follow will help you assess what you already know or believe about work-life balance. Rate how well each statement describes you right now on a scale from 1 to 5, with 1 representing "not at all" and 5 representing "to a great extent." Use the space below each statement to make any notes that would explain your response.

My work and personal lives are well balanced.   1   2   3   4   5

_____

_____

_____

I believe that balanced leaders are more effective.   1   2   3   4   5

_____

_____

_____

Work-life balance is an obtainable goal for me.
     1   2   3   4   5

_____

_____

_____

I have a good understanding of the ways in which my work affects my personal life and vice versa.
     1   2   3   4   5

_____

_____

_____

My work affects my personal life in a positive way.
     1   2   3   4   5

_____

_____

_____

My work affects my personal life in a negative way
     1   2   3   4   5

_____

_____

_____

My personal life affects my work life in a positive way.   1   2   3   4   5

_____

_____

_____

My personal life affects my work life in a negative way.   1   2   3   4   5

_____

_____

_____

Lack of work-life balance affects my daily mood,   1   2   3   4   5
productivity, or sleep patterns.

_____

_____

_____

What are the implications of your ratings for you as a leader? What are you pleased about? What are you concerned about?

_____

_____

_____

_____

_____

EXPLORE THE TOPIC

The questions and activities in this section will help you discover the ways in which your personal and work lives affect one another, assess the costs and benefits of that interdependency, and come up with strategies for achieving your desired work-life balance.

1. Take a few minutes to think about your life: your day-to-day tasks, your relationships, your commitments and obligations, and the people, activities, places, and other things you enjoy. Then, using the My Life Now space on the following page, a whiteboard, or a separate sheet of paper, set a timer for five minutes, and do *one* of the following:

- Write down every word or phrase that occurs to you that describes your life right now. Don't stop to think, and don't censor (cross out) anything.
- Draw a picture or an abstract image that expresses your life right now. Don't worry about your artistic skills. Give yourself permission to draw like a four-year-old.
- Write a letter to someone you trust completely, describing your life right now. Tell the person what you do and how you feel about what you do. Start writing as soon as you set the timer, and keep writing until it goes off. Don't stop to think, and don't censor what you write.

MY LIFE NOW

Now look at the results. Circle words, phrases, and images that are key to your current state of work-life balance or imbalance. Then answer these questions:

• What surprised you about what you wrote?

_____

_____

_____

• What patterns did you discover?

_____

_____

_____

• What is working about your work-life balance right now? What is not working?

_____

_____

_____

2. In Chapter Two, you considered the question, "Given the costs of leadership, is being a leader worth the time and effort?" But at least some of the costs may also have some corresponding benefits. For example, although the travel your work requires may take you away from your family, it can offer important experiences and help you develop relationships that can serve both your career and your personal life. Taking on the increased responsibility of a new leadership position might lead to more daily stress, but it might also provide increased income that helps you achieve financial goals.

In the list that follows of possible costs and benefits, check those that seem relevant to your situation. Add any that are relevant for you but not on the list. Please note that while these costs and benefits are presented in the form of a dichotomy (that is, you have either one or the other), in reality, the lines between costs and benefits are usually blurred. Checking the boxes in this exercise is simply a way to prompt your thinking about what's working and not working for you right now.

Possible costs

☐ Physical energy

☐ Mental energy

☐ Spiritual energy

☐ Long hours at work

☐ Time spent in meetings

☐ Constant obligations

☐ Responsibility

☐ Caretaking requirements of family members

☐ Less time for nonleadership work interests

☐ Visibility (being in a fishbowl)

☐ Public duties

☐ Isolation from peers

☐ Less freedom of expression

☐ Pressure to produce

☐ Stress on family

☐ Less time for family

☐ Less time for other pursuits

☐ Emotional strains

☐ Very little feedback from boss

☐ Unhelpful feedback from boss

☐ Too much travel

☐ Bad relocations

☐ Job insecurity

☐ Other (specify):

☐ Other (specify):

☐ Other (specify):

☐ Other (specify):

☐ Other (specify):

☐ Other (specify):

Possible benefits

☐ Physical energy

☐ Mental energy

☐ Spiritual energy

☐ Pride of accomplishment

☐ Financial rewards

☐ Self-validation and opportunities to change and grow

☐ Impact on people and events; inclusion of others in the leadership journey

☐ Responsibility

☐ Service to others

☐ Meaning and respect from others

☐ Attention and recognition

☐ Visibility

☐ Personal prominence

☐ New connections and acquaintances

☐ Helping others grow

☐ Perks of position

☐ More financial resources for family

☐ Personal status

☐ Singular achievements; personal control

☐ Heightened experience

☐ More autonomy

☐ Travel linked to recreation

☐ Self-analysis of personal and career priorities and ultimately a job or life change

☐ Other (specify):

☐ Other (specify):

☐ Other (specify):   ☐ Other (specify):

☐ Other (specify):

☐ Other (specify):

☐ Other (specify):

☐ Other (specify):

After checking the costs and benefits that are relevant to your situation, how would you summarize what's working and what's not working for you?

_____

_____

_____

_____

_____

3. Roles outside work provide lessons we can use as leaders. What roles do you hold outside work? Check them on the list that follows, and add any that are not listed. For each role that you check, briefly describe the demands on you of the role and some key insights or skills you have learned that are useful in your role as a leader.

☐ *Son or daughter*
Demands of this role:

_____

_____

_____

Lessons learned from this role:

_____

_____

_____

☐ *Sibling*
Demands of this role:

_____

_____

_____

Lessons learned from this role:

_____

_____

_____

☐ *Spouse or partner*
Demands of this role:

_____

_____

_____

Lessons learned from this role:

_____

_____

_____

☐ *Parent*
Demands of this role:

_____

_____

_____

Lessons learned from this role:

_____

_____

_____

☐ *Friend*
Demands of this role:

_____

_____

_____

Lessons learned from this role:

_____

_____

_____

☐ *Neighbor*
Demands of this role:

_____

_____

_____

Lessons learned from this role:

_____

_____

_____

☐ *Coach*
Demands of this role:

_____

_____

_____

Lessons learned from this role:

_____

_____

_____

☐ *Advocate*
Demands of this role:

_____

_____

_____

Lessons learned from this role:

_____

_____

_____

☐ *Volunteer*
Demands of this role:

_____

_____

_____

Lessons learned from this role:

_____

_____

_____

☐ Other_____
Demands of this role:

_____

_____

_____

Lessons learned from this role:

_____

_____

_____

☐ Other_____
Demands of this role:

_____

_____

_____

Lessons learned from this role:

_____

_____

_____

☐ Other_____

Demands of this role:

_____

_____

_____

Lessons learned from this role:

_____

_____

_____

Identify which lessons are valuable to you as a leader. How will you use them more? How are these different roles synergistic with each other?

_____

_____

_____

_____

Now, go back to the roles listed in Chapter Five (Facilitator, Coach, Negotiator). Pick each role that you play at work, and describe the lessons you have learned from being in these roles. How might these lessons benefit you in your personal life? How will you use them?

_____

_____

_____

4. The descriptions of strategies to help you achieve better work-life balance are provided in the Five Strategies for Achieving Work-Life Balance chart. Check the appropriate column to the right of each strategy to indicate whether you have tried to use it, are currently using it, or haven't tried it. In the space below each strategy, note the results of the strategies you have tried or are currently using and what you think the strategies you haven't tried might help you accomplish.

Note: Before you complete the chart, take another look at your response at the end of activity 1 (p. 97) about what is and is not working right now in your work-life balance. Take another few moments to think about that question and jot a few more notes in your workbook, in your journal, or on another sheet of paper. After completing the chart, go back to your notes and add other insights you may have.

FIVE STRATEGIES FOR ACHIEVING WORK-LIFE BALANCE

Strategy	Have tried	Now using	Haven't tried
Integrating: Identifying what you really want in each area of your life and designing a space in which you can accomplish those goals in an integrated way			
Narrowing: Deciding to "clean your mental closet" by delegating or dropping certain tasks, goals, expectations, relationships, commitments, and obligations and by making choices so that you can focus on what's really important to you			
Moderating: Spending the right amount of time in each area of your life instead of trying to do everything perfectly			
Sequencing: Setting priorities and deciding what to do first, second, and so on, so that you can achieve your goals			
Adding resources: Identifying and finding the resources you need to accomplish your work more quickly and to manage multiple priorities			

5. On a separate sheet of paper, a whiteboard, or your computer, list twenty things you love to do (for example, play tennis, read, travel, dine with friends, play with your children, hike in the wilderness, read a good mystery novel, do volunteer work, play music). Focus on what gives you energy and joy, not on what other people expect of you or what you think they expect of you. When you're finished, consider these questions:

   • Did anything surprise you?

   • Which of the values that you identified in Chapter Three are represented in the activities you listed?

   • What would it take for you to be able to make more time for these activities?

EXPAND YOUR LEARNING

The activities that follow can help you learn more about your personal realities, demands, and expectations and the ways in which they affect you as a leader. Note your observations and responses in your leadership journal.

1. Inventory how you spend your time. Keep a detailed log for two weeks. Record everything you do at work and in your personal life, and indicate how long each task and activity takes. Be as detailed as possible; include giving your children their evening baths, working out at the gym, going to a sports event or the theater, cooking meals, visiting with friends, writing a report, talking with clients on the phone, conducting a hiring interview, and facilitating a team meeting, for example. When the two weeks are up, go through your log and reflect on these questions:

   • Which activities were necessary for daily living? For your career? Your family and friends? Your health? Your well-being?

   • What percentage of time did you spend in work-related activities, family activities, and with friends to maintain your health and well-being?

   • Did you spend enough time on activities that inspire and energize you?

   • What proportion of time did you spend on must-do activities? Nice-to-do but not essential activities? Activities that could be handed off to someone else? Activities that did not really need to be done at all?

- Were there instances where your interests created conflict and a sense of internal competition within yourself? (For example, is your quest to be a better golfer driven by the desire to conduct more business or by the love of the game—or both? Does your desire to become more technologically proficient so that you can get more done at work conflict with a family value of being present at your child's concert?)

- What are the key insights you draw from this activity relative to how you actually spend your time and how you would like to spend your time?

2. Use the Stress Assessment activity, adapted from *Managing Leadership Stress* (Bal, Campbell, & McDowell-Larsen, 2008), to help you recognize your negative responses to stress.

STRESS ASSESSMENT

Many leaders operate in continually high-pressure environments, so they often don't recognize their negative responses to stress. But because long-term consequences of stressful situations can be detrimental to your health and well-being, it is important that you identify when your reactions don't help alleviate the stress that you feel. Consider the following descriptions of common stress reactions. How often do these descriptions match your responses?

Ticking Time Bomb

Early signs: Doesn't acknowledge low levels of stress. Lets stressful events pass. Swallows his initial reaction to stressors.

Consequence: Takes on more and more work and responsibility. No one around him knows that he is stressed.

Over time: More and more he sends signs of distress, such as an angry comment, refusing to help a colleague, withholding information.

The end: Eventually, he explodes with an emotional outburst. His resources for handling stress decrease because he damages his relationships with others.

I have seen this in myself:

☐ Often

☐ Sometimes

☐ Seldom

The Critic

Early signs: Picks at the details unnecessarily. Finds something negative in just about everything. Makes small critical comments that may be couched in humor as sarcasm.

Consequence: Her negative behavior keeps people at a distance and decreases her access to social support.

Over time: A pall of negativity affects the working climate of the group or team and has a negative impact on its productivity.

The end: Eventually, the negativity bruises and batters what could have been effective relationships. Her stress increases because of a lack of social support.

I have seen this in myself:

☐ Often

☐ Sometimes

☐ Seldom

The Self-Indulgent Monster

Early signs: Not able to focus on work. Distracts himself with other, less important tasks. Unable to remain productive.

Consequence: Feels guilty about his lack of productivity. His negative self-image adds to the stress he feels.

Over time: He retreats into himself and continues to distract himself with sensory pursuits like watching TV, drinking alcohol to excess, and overeating.

The end: Eventually, his sensory pursuits detract from his ability to cope, and interfere with his recovery from the stressful situation.

I have seen this in myself:

☐ Often

☐ Sometimes

☐ Seldom

(continued)

The Ulcer Giver

Early signs: Gives undue negative feedback to others. Passes stressful tasks on to others and takes on an "If I have to suffer, so should they" attitude.

Consequence: Her behavior alienates others, and it also creates stress for them.

Over time: The productivity of entire groups and departments in which she plays a role starts to erode.

The end: Her frustration, brought on by stress and her inability to alleviate it, emerge as aggressive behavior toward others.

I have seen this in myself:

☐ Often

☐ Sometimes

☐ Seldom

The Yes Man

Early signs: Not fazed by stress. Maintains positive working relationships. Takes on more and more tasks and claims to thrive under stress.

Consequence: Others see him as being able to handle inhuman amounts of work, so he gets more work.

Over time: Continues to accumulate more work, more responsibility.

The end: Eventually turns into a ticking time bomb, a critic, a self-indulgent monster, or an ulcer giver.

I have seen this in myself:

☐ Often

☐ Sometimes

☐ Seldom

THEMES AND PATTERNS

Pull together what you have learned in this chapter about your personal realities, demands, and expectations and their relationship to your leadership:

1. Having done the activities in this chapter, how clear are you on your work-life balance—what it means for you to achieve the right amount of focus, energy, and time across the many areas of your life?

_____Very clear   _____Somewhat clear   _____Not very clear

If you answered "not very clear" to this question, you might want to continue exploring the topic by consulting some of the resources listed at the end of the book.

2. Reflect on your responses to the questions in this chapter. Then write a six-word story that expresses what you have learned in this chapter about your work-life balance and its impact on you as a leader. (As an alternative, write six words that summarize the major takeaway points or learning from the chapter.)

_____ _____ _____ _____ _____ _____

3. What other insights have you had from this chapter?

_____

_____

_____

4. Write a one- to two-paragraph letter to yourself about the ways in which your personal realities, demands, and expectations affect your role as a leader. Address the following:

• What an ideal balanced life looks like for you

• Actions you can take to better manage the tensions between your work and your personal life so that you can be a more effective leader

LETTER TO MYSELF

NOW WHAT?

What will you do to use what you have learned in this chapter? Which actions can you take immediately? Which actions require the help of others? Whose help do you need? What can you do to get it?

Action	Can take now? Yes or No?	Requires help from	To get help, I will

What do you still need to explore and understand about your work-life balance and its connection to your leadership?

_____

_____

_____

WHAT'S NEXT?

In the previous chapters of this workbook, you have explored each of the five components of the Discovering Leadership Framework. In the final chapter, you will pull together everything that you have learned, develop an action plan for moving forward in your leadership role, and think about the implications of what you have discovered for the future decisions you make about your leadership.

CHAPTER SEVEN

ACTION PLANNING

Your development as a leader is not an event; it is an ongoing, even lifelong process that requires continuing self-examination and attention. It is complex, and it can get messy. As you move forward in your career, things will change, and you may often find yourself in a state of drift that requires returning to the self-discovery process to get back on track.

The Discovering Leadership Framework that you have learned to use in this workbook is a tool for expanding and extending the discovery process and working through important decisions about your leadership role. You may return to the framework, or parts of it, again and again as you face important choices or find the way ahead blocked in some way. As we noted in the Preface, we also recommend that you purchase the *Discovering the Leader in You* book, which can give you more insight into the material contained in this workbook. (Visit www.ccl.org for more information.)

Keep in mind that you should not make your journey alone. You can benefit from the help of many other people—coaches, mentors, role models, colleagues, significant others, friends, and others—who can offer you honest feedback, help you consider different perspectives, provide you with new information and ideas, help you explore your feelings about your work, and help you feel validated and encouraged.

To keep moving forward in a way that increases your chances of success, however, you need an action plan. A useful action plan includes measurable development goals and specific actions for achieving them, a timetable, resources you need to achieve goals, potential obstacles and strategies for dealing with them, and a monitoring plan. The action plan should also identify development partners who can provide support and feedback as you take steps to achieve your goals. The two copies of the Action Planning Worksheet in this chapter will help you prepare your action plans.

WHAT'S IN THIS CHAPTER?

The questions and activities in this chapter will help you:

- Reflect on what you learned in each chapter of this workbook so you can consolidate and synthesize the themes and patterns you discovered

- Clarify your purpose for being a leader and the ways in which leadership fits into your life and decide how best to make major decisions about taking on or continuing in leadership roles

- Think about your hopes and dreams for yourself as a leader, clarify your goals, and identify people who can help you reach what you hope to achieve

- Develop an action plan for achieving goals that focuses on specific areas of change (for example, seeking a new developmental assignment, developing more balance, further developing your leadership vision, determining whether to pursue a specific leadership role)

- Continually assess how you are doing on your leadership journey

LEARNING OBJECTIVES

When you complete this chapter, you will be able to:

- Articulate clearly and concisely who you are as a leader and your purpose for leading

- Clarify specific goals for furthering your development as a leader

- Develop an action plan for achieving goals that meets the criteria set forth in the chapter

YOUR CURRENT STATE

How clear are you on the elements of the Discovering Leadership Framework? To assess what you have learned about yourself as a leader through your work in Chapters One through Six, review those chapters and the notes you have made in your leadership journal. Rate yourself on how well the following statements apply to you using the following scale:

1 = Not at all   2 = Not very well   3 = Well   4 = Moderately well
5 = Very well

_____ I can describe aspects of my organization's culture as well as the organizational challenges and trends that have the most impact on me as a leader (Chapter Two).

_____ I have a good understanding of my primary view, perspective, or philosophy of leadership (Chapter Two).

_____ I have a good understanding of the ways in which my organization rewards certain styles or philosophies of leadership (Chapter Two).

_____ I can identify specific costs of leadership that might contribute to my sense of leadership drift now or in the future (Chapter Two).

_____ I have a good understanding of why a clear, compelling leadership vision is foundational to my ability to be a successful leader (Chapter Three).

_____ I can clearly articulate my leadership vision and describe how it is connected to my personal vision (Chapter Three).

_____ I clearly understand the importance of making conscious choices to align my vision and the work I do (Chapter Three).

_____ I can identify my top core values and how they play out in my behavior as a leader (Chapter Four).

_____ I have a good understanding of what motivates me to be a leader (Chapter Four).

_____ I understand the importance of aligning my values, motivations, and the work I do (Chapter Four).

_____ I recognize the connections between my leadership vision and my values (Chapter Four).

_____ I have a good understanding of when, where, and how I prefer to lead (Chapter Five).

_____ I can describe my strengths and weak areas on each of the six elements of my leadership profile (Chapter Five).

_____ I can describe the ways in which my life and work experiences have helped to make me the leader I am today (Chapter Five).

_____ I have a good idea about issues that might lead me to derail as I move forward in my career (Chapter Five).

_____ I have a clear understanding of the interdependencies between my personal and work lives (Chapter Six).

_____ I can describe the ways in which the tensions and conflicts between my personal and work lives are connected and can lead to stress (Chapter Six).

_____ I have a good idea about the kinds of changes I need to make to achieve my optimum work-life balance and how to go about making those changes (Chapter Six).

If you rated any items a 3 or below, you might want to go back and take another look at your work on that chapter. To expand your learning about the topic, you might also want to read or re-read the *Discovering the Leader in You* Book.

CONSOLIDATING THEMES AND PATTERNS

Follow the steps to consolidate and deepen your understanding of the themes and patterns you have discovered through this workbook.

1. What have you learned about yourself as a leader by answering the questions and doing the activities in this workbook? Use the Discovering Leadership Framework in Figure 7.1 to pull together your most salient ideas, observations, and insights. For each of the five areas of the framework, review the corresponding chapter in the workbook, as well as the notes in your leadership journal. Then write key words and phrases that express the most important things you learned in relationship to each component of the framework. Figure 7.2 provides an example.

When you are finished, review what you wrote and consider the following:

• What themes and patterns consistently emerge?

_____

_____

_____

FIGURE 7.1 Discovering Leadership Framework

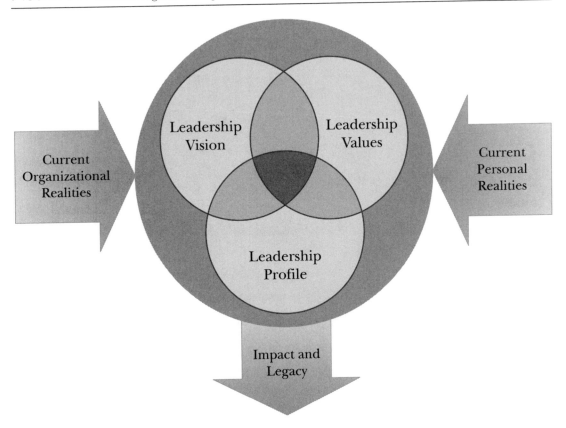

- Does anything surprise you? If so, what?

_____

_____

_____

- What connections do you see?

_____

_____

_____

FIGURE 7.2 A Real-World Example

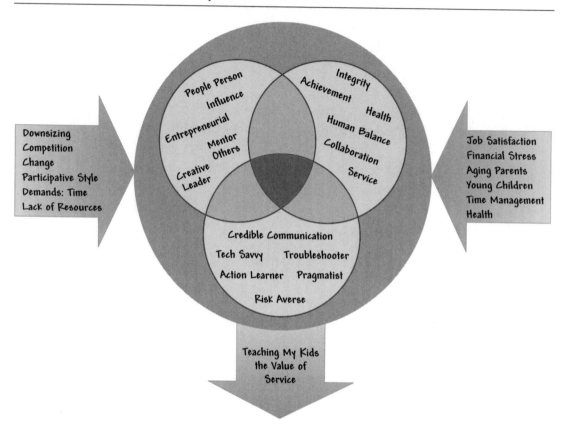

- What conflicts do you see?

  _____

  _____

  _____

- Are there elements that still aren't clear for you? If so, what are they?

  _____

  _____

  _____

2. Think about your leadership vision, your core values, and your key strengths. Imagine that a journalist who is writing about a selected group of leaders asks you, "What do you want to accomplish as a leader? What difference would you like to make? What legacy would you like to leave?"

Here are examples of responses that other leaders have given to that question:

"I want to start a new program for underprivileged children."

"I want our company to be recognized for providing the best customer service in our industry."

"I want to develop the talent capacity in our organization to meet the challenges we face in the next three to five years in a way that we are perceived as best-in-class."

"I want to lead my team in the development of innovations that will help to reduce our impact on the environment."

"I want to become president of my division in order to have the influence and impact I envision."

"I want to lead the corporate philanthropy efforts in our organization."

How would *you* respond to the journalist's question? Jot down some key words and phrases on these lines:

_____

_____

_____

_____

_____

Take some time to reflect on what you have written. Then write a one- to three-sentence statement that expresses the essence of what you want to accomplish as a leader:

_____

_____

_____

3. At the ends of Chapters Two through Six of this workbook, you wrote brief letters to yourself about what you had learned in that chapter. Read those letters again. Underline or highlight anything that leaps out at you as important to your leader discovery process.

Now use the Looking to the Future space here (or a page in your leadership journal) to write something—a letter, a poem, a journal entry, or another form of writing—that expresses where you would like to go from here and how you think you could get there. What are your goals as a leader? What do you want to continue doing? What new things do you want to do? What steps could you take to achieve your goals? Who are some people who can help you along the way?

LOOKING TO THE FUTURE

_____

_____

_____

_____

_____

_____

_____

_____

_____

_____

_____

_____

_____

No matter what form of writing you use, write a quick first draft without stopping to think and without censoring yourself. Then go back and read what you have written. Have you left anything important out? Does anything need to be clarified? Make any revisions needed so that the piece of writing expresses clearly your hopes and desires as a leader, includes your goals and steps for reaching them, and identifies some people who can help you on your journey.

4. Throughout this workbook, you have been writing six-word stories to capture your most important insights on a specific topic or for a particular chapter. Now write a new six-word story that captures the essence of who you are as a leader. (As an alternative, write six words that capture that essence.)

_____ _____ _____ _____ _____ _____

5. Imagine that you have been offered an interview for your ideal leadership opportunity, and the interview is to take place tomorrow. Take another look at the Discovering Leadership Framework in Figure 7.1 that you filled out, at your letters to yourself, and at any other relevant notes you have made in this workbook. Then think about why this is the ideal leadership opportunity for you and write down the critical things you want the interviewer to know about you.

*Why this is an ideal
leadership opportunity*   *My critical competencies*

_____   _____

_____   _____

_____   _____

_____   _____

_____   _____

6. Support and help on your leadership journey can come from many different people. Use the following activity, adapted from *Three Keys to Development: Defining and Meeting Your Leadership Challenges* (Browning & Van Velsor, 1999), to prepare to seek the right support from the right people. Think about what formal and informal roles you need supporters to play. Some helpful support roles include the following:

Informal roles

- *Counselor:* Provides emotional support and encouragement and lets you vent your feelings
- *Cheerleader:* Expresses confidence in your current abilities and your ability to learn and grow
- *Reinforcer:* Rewards you for your progress
- *Cohort:* As someone in a situation similar to yours, can offer empathy

Formal roles

- *Mentor:* Provides long-term support and guidance through experience and example
- *Coach:* Provides focused support to help you acquire a specific skill or overcome a particular hurdle; ensures that you get ongoing assessment and feedback on your progress

Which of the support roles described above would be useful to you now and during the next stages of your journey? Who might fill each of those roles for you?

Challenge or area for improvement:

_____

Support roles:

_____Counselor   _____Cheerleader   _____Reinforcer   _____Cohort
_____Mentor   _____Coach

Potential person to fill that role:

_____

Challenge or area for improvement:

_____

Support roles:

_____Counselor   _____Cheerleader   _____Reinforcer   _____Cohort
_____Mentor   _____Coach

Potential person to fill that role:

_____

Challenge or area for improvement:

_____

Support roles:

_____Counselor   _____Cheerleader   _____Reinforcer   _____Cohort
_____Mentor   _____Coach

Potential person to fill that role:

_____

ACTION PLANNING

Change is often best accomplished by working on one or two goals at a time. Here we include two action planning worksheets you can use to pull together everything you have learned and to develop an action plan for moving forward toward two goals. Your goals should meet the following SMART criteria:

Be specific. Describe your goals—exactly what you want to accomplish—in as much detail as possible.

Be measurable. Identify quantifiable targets for tracking your progress and results.

Be attainable. Make sure that it is possible to achieve the desired results.

Be realistic. Make sure that the necessary resources, including time, can be available.

Be timed. Specify deadlines for each activity and for reaching the goal.

ACTION PLANNING WORKSHEET

My goal _____ Start Date: _____

Measurable Activities: What I must do to achieve goal	Accountability: Person to whom I am accountable for each activity	Timed Activities: Date and times for each activity	Available Resources: Internal and external
Evaluation Process: Methods for measuring progress	Benefits that will accrue	Commitment: Obstacles to overcome	Sacrifices that will be required

ACTION PLANNING WORKSHEET

My goal _____   Start Date: _____

Measurable Activities: What I must do to achieve goal	**Accountability:** Person to whom I am accountable for each activity	**Timed Activities:** Date and times for each activity	**Available Resources:** Internal and external
Evaluation Process: Methods for measuring progress	**Commitment:** Benefits that will accrue	**Commitment:** Obstacles to overcome	Sacrifices that will be required

CONTINUE YOUR DEVELOPMENT

As we mentioned earlier in this workbook, leadership development is an ongoing process. Following are two activities that can help you build on what you have learned.

1. Seek what Marshall Goldsmith (2002) calls "feedforward" from others by doing the following:

- Pick a behavior that you would like to change. Choose a behavior that should make a significant, positive difference in someone's life.
- Describe this behavior to a colleague or a friend.
- Ask for suggestions that might help you achieve a positive change in the behavior you selected.
- As you proceed toward your goals, repeat this process with other behaviors you wish to change.

2. As you move forward in your career, you will find yourself faced with important decisions about your leadership. The leadership decision ladder in Figure 7.3 provides a systematic way to make those decisions. The ladder embodies

FIGURE 7.3 Leadership Decision Ladder

similar questions as those in the Discovering Leadership Framework, but it presents them in a different order and with a different perspective.

Each of the ladder's five rungs represents a point of connection between leadership choices you have made in the past and the context surrounding those choices. In thinking about how you relate to this ladder, you may find that you are moving up the ladder toward more leadership responsibility in a relatively concerted way or that you have paused on one of the rungs as you postpone further leadership commitments. You might conclude that the view you have from the rung you're on is just right; staying where you are provides you with what you need at a particular point in time. Think about a decision that you will or may need to make about whether to pursue a specific leadership opportunity. Then ascend the rungs of the leadership decision ladder by considering these questions:

Rung 1. Grounding yourself. Think about your personal vision, values, and competencies. At your core, who are you, and how do these core factors affect you as a leader? How does this new opportunity fit with those core factors?

Rung 2. Developing a vision. Think about your vision for leadership—what you want to accomplish and how being a leader will help you. How will this new leadership opportunity help you accomplish your purpose in life?

Rung 3. Engaging challenge. Think about the new things about leadership that you would like to learn or try. Will this new leadership opportunity allow you the growth, learning, and experimentation that you need to improve your skills?

Rung 4. Accounting for others. Think about what you want to accomplish for and with others or for an organization. How will seizing this opportunity help advance or fulfill these larger goals? How will others benefit from your leadership and help achieve the changes you desire? Considering the available resources and support, as well as the job context and responsibility, how realistic is what you hope to accomplish?

Rung 5. Picking your time. Think about your personal context and the demands of the new leadership position. Is this the right time for you to take on a new or expanded opportunity? What will be the benefits and trade-offs? Will this opportunity open up the possibility of another opportunity that you think you might want? Will saying yes or no now limit your options later?

CLOSING

As we said at the beginning of this workbook, discovering the leader in you is a lifelong process. In fact, if you ever get to the point where you think you have figured out how to be an exemplary leader, it's probably time to retire. The best leaders commit themselves to continual learning and improving their skills hour by hour and day by day. We wrote our book and this workbook to help you do just that: improve your skills so that you can unleash your own talents and those of others to help make a difference in the world. We wish you much success in taking these ideas and converting them into concrete actions.

READINGS AND RESOURCES

Chapter One

Criswell, C., & Campbell, D. (2008). *Building an authentic leadership image*. Greensboro, NC: Center for Creative Leadership.

Csikszentmihalyi, M. (1990). *Flow: The psychology of optimal experience*. New York: HarperCollins.

Gergen, C., & Vanourek, G. (2008). *Life entrepreneurs: Ordinary people creating extraordinary lives*. San Francisco: Jossey-Bass.

George, B., Sims, P., McLean, A. N., & Mayer, D. (2007). Discovering your authentic leadership. *Harvard Business Review*, *85*(2), 129–138.

Goldsmith, M., & Reiter, M. (2009). *Mojo: How to get it, how to keep it, how to get it back if you lose it*. New York: Hyperion.

Kaplan, R. S. (2007). What to ask the person in the mirror. *Harvard Business Review*, *85*(1), 86–96.

Ruderman, M. N., & Ohlott, P. J. (2000). *Learning from life: Turning life's lessons into leadership experience*. Greensboro, NC: Center for Creative Leadership.

Wei, R., & Yip, J. (2008). *Leadership wisdom: Discovering the lessons of experience*. Greensboro, NC: Center for Creative Leadership.

Chapter Two

Bunker, K. A. (2008). *Responses to change: Helping people manage transition*. Greensboro, NC: Center for Creative Leadership.

Christensen, C. M. (2010). How will you measure your life? *Harvard Business Review*, *88*(7/8), 46–51.

Deal, J., & Prince, D. (2003). *Developing cultural adaptability: How to work across differences*. Greensboro, NC: Center for Creative Leadership.

de Meuse, K. P., Tang, K. Y., Mlodzik, K. J., & Dai, G. (2010). *The world is flat . . . and so are leadership competencies*. Los Angeles: Korn/Ferry International. Retrieved Aug. 24, 2010, from http://www.kornferryinstitute.com/ebook/2203/pdf1/The_World_is_Flat_June_2010.pdf

Ernst, C., & Yip, J. (2008). Bridging boundaries: Meeting the challenge of workplace diversity. *Leadership in Action, 28*(10), 3–7.

Gitsham, M., Lenssen, L., Quinn, L., de Bettignies, H. C., Gomez, J., & Oliver-Evans, C. (2008). *Developing the global leader of tomorrow.* Ashridge, UK: Ashridge. Retrieved Aug. 24, 2010, from http://www.unprme.org/resource-docs/DevelopingTheGlobalLeaderOfTomorrowReport.pdf

Heifetz, R., Grashow, A., & Linsky, M. (2009). Leadership in a (permanent) crisis. *Harvard Business Review, 87*(7/8), 62–69.

McGuire, J. B., & Rhodes, G. B. (2009). *Transforming your leadership culture.* San Francisco: Jossey-Bass and Center for Creative Leadership.

McKinsey & Company. (2009). *McKinsey Global survey results: Leadership through the crisis and after.* Washington, DC: Author. Retrieved Aug. 24, 2010, from http://www.mckinseyquarterly.com/Leadership_through_the_crisis_and_after_McKinsey_Global_Survey_results_2457

Perrin, C., Blauth, C., Apthorp, E., Daniels, S., Marone, M., Thompsen, J., et al. (2010). *Developing the 21st-century leader: A multi-level analysis of global trends in leadership challenges and practices.* Tampa, FL: Achieve Global. http://www.achieveglobal.com/resources/files/AchieveGlobal_21st_Century_Leader_Report.pdf

Chapter Three

Cartwright, T., & Baldwin, D. (2006). *Communicating your vision.* Greensboro, NC: Center for Creative Leadership.

Criswell, C., & Cartwright, T. (2010). *Creating a vision.* Greensboro, NC: Center for Creative Leadership.

Guber, P. (2007). The four truths of the storyteller. *Harvard Business Review, 85*(12), 52–59.

Ibarra, H. (2010). Women and the vision thing. *Harvard Business Review, 87*(1), 62–70.

Ibarra, H., & Lineback, K. (2005). What's your story? *Harvard Business Review, 83*(1), 64–71.

LaChapelle, C. (2004). *Finding your voice, telling your stories: 167 ways to tell your life stories.* Portland, OR: Marion Street Press.

Chapter Four

Boyatzis, R., McKee, A., & Goldman, D. (2002). Reawakening your passion for work. *Harvard Business Review, 80*(4), 86–94.

Cartwright, T. (2007). *Setting priorities: Personal values, organizational results.* Greensboro, NC: Center for Creative Leadership.

Criswell, C., & Campbell, D. (2009, Apr.). Authentic leadership: The importance of being authentic. *Human Resources,* 20–26.

Goffee, R., & Jones, G. (2005). Managing authenticity: The paradox of great leadership. *Harvard Business Review, 83*(12), 86–94.

Hannum, K. M. (2007). *Social identity: Knowing yourself, leading others*. Greensboro, NC: Center for Creative Leadership.

Hannum, K., McFeeters, B. B., & Booysen, L. (2010). *Leading across differences: Facilitator's guide set*. San Francisco: Jossey-Bass/Pfeiffer.

Hannum, K., McFeeters, B. B., & Booysen, L. (2010). *Leading across differences: Casebook*. San Francisco: Jossey-Bass/Pfeiffer.

Hesselbein, F., & Goldsmith, M. (2006). *The leader of the future: Visions, strategies and practices for the new era*. San Francisco: Jossey-Bass.

Wrzesniewski, A., Berg, J. M., & Dutton, J. E. (2010). Turn the job you have into the job you want. *Harvard Business Review, 88*(6), 114–117.

Chapter Five

Bolman, L. G., & Deal, T. E. (2009). Battles and beliefs: Rethinking the *roles* of today's leaders. *Leadership in Action, 29*(5), 14–18.

Chappelow, C. T., & Leslie, J. B. (2001). *Keeping your career on track: Twenty success strategies*. Greensboro, NC: Center for Creative Leadership.

Calarco, A., & Gurvis, J. (2006). *Adaptability: Responding effectively to change*. Greensboro, NC: Center for Creative Leadership.

Dalton, M. (1998). *Becoming a more versatile learner*. Greensboro, NC: Center for Creative Leadership.

Gentry, W. A., Mondore, S. P., & Cox, B. D. (2007). A study of managerial derailment characteristics and personality preferences. *Journal of Management Development, 26*(9), 857–873.

Leslie, J. B. (2009). *Leadership gap: What you need, and don't have, when it comes to leadership talent*. Greensboro, NC: Center for Creative Leadership. Retrieved Aug. 26, 2010, from http://www.ccl.org/leadership/pdf/research/leadershipGap.pdf

Lombardo, M. M., & Eichinger, R. W. (2009). *FYI: For your improvement: A guide for development and coaching: for learners, managers, mentors, and feedback givers* (5th ed.). Minneapolis, MN: Lominger.

McCauley, C. D. (2006). *Developmental assignments: Creating learning experiences without changing jobs*. Greensboro, NC: Center for Creative Leadership.

Chapter Six

Bal, V., Campbell, M., & McDowell-Larsen, S. (2008). *Managing leadership stress*. Greensboro, NC: Center for Creative Leadership.

Bird, J. (2006). Balance requires evolving skills. *T+D, 60*(5), 66–67.

Conlin, M. (Ed.). (2008, Aug. 14). Work-life balance: How to get a life and do your job. *BusinessWeek*. Retrieved Aug. 27, 2010, from http://www.businessweek.com/magazine/content/08_34/b4097036727134.htm

Friedman, S. D. (2008). Be a better leader, have a richer life. *Harvard Business Review, 86*(4), 112–118.

Gurvis, J., & Patterson, G. (2004). *Finding your balance.* Greensboro, NC: Center for Creative Leadership.

Gurvis, J., & Patterson, G. (2005). Balancing act: Finding equilibrium between work and life. *Leadership in Action, 24*(6), 3–8.

Hannum, K. M. (2007). *Social identity: Knowing yourself, leading others.* Greensboro, NC: Center for Creative Leadership.

Hollingsworth, M. (2005). Resolving the dilemma of work-life balance: Developing life-maps. *Ivey Business Journal, 70*(2), 1–8.

Murray, K. (2010). Balancing work and life. *Personal Excellence, 15*(4), 8.

Ruderman, M. N., & Ernst, C. (2010). Finding yourself: How social identity affects leadership. *Leadership in Action, 30*(1), 14–18.

Schwartz, T. (2007). Manage your energy, not your time. *Harvard Business Review, 85*(10), 63–73.

Chapter Seven

Ancona, D., Malone, T. W., Orlikowski, W. J., & Senge, P. M. (2007). In praise of the incomplete leader. *Harvard Business Review, 85*(2), 92–100.

Browning, H., & Van Velsor, E. (1999). *Three keys to development: Defining and meeting your leadership challenges.* Greensboro, NC: Center for Creative Leadership.

Ensher, E. A., & Murphy, S. E. (2005). *Power mentoring: How successful mentors and protégés get the most out of their relationships.* San Francisco: Jossey-Bass.

George, B., & Sims, P. (2007). *True North: Discover your authentic leadership.* San Francisco: Jossey-Bass.

Goldsmith, M. (2002). Try feedforward instead of feedback. Retrieved Jan. 10, 2011, from http://www.marshallgoldsmithlibrary.com/cim/articles_display.php?aid=110

Heffernan, M., & Joni, S. N. (2005, Aug.). Of protégés and pitfalls. *Fast Company,* pp. 81–84. Retrieved Aug. 27, 2010, from http://www.fastcompany.com/magazine/97/open_playbook.html

Kaplan, R. S. (2008). Reaching your potential. *Harvard Business Review, 86*(7/8), 45–49.

Sternbergh, W. W., & Weitzel, S. R. (2001). *Setting your development goals: Start with your values.* Greensboro, NC: Center for Creative Leadership.

ABOUT THE AUTHORS

SARA N. KING, principal of Optimum Insights, Inc., helps leaders explore their potential and increase their performance through her expertise as an executive coach, keynote speaker, author, workshop designer, and facilitator. During twenty-five years in leadership development, she has served thousands of executives in Fortune 500 companies, government agencies, educational institutions, and nonprofits. Throughout two decades at the Center for Creative Leadership, Sara held roles as a global executive, trainer, program manager, and researcher. She began her extensive work in the field of women's leadership in 1986 as a member of the Breaking the Glass Ceiling research team, which studied the career development of executive women in Fortune 100 firms. That team produced the 1987 book *Breaking the Glass Ceiling: Can Women Reach the Top of America's Largest Corporations?* by Ann Morrison, Randall White, and Ellen Van Velsor. Sara's passion for women's leadership includes her eighteen-year relationship with the national Women in Cable Telecommunications organization, where she is a facilitator in the flagship leadership program. Sara earned her B.A. in English from Wake Forest University and an M.S. in higher education administration from Cornell University. She serves on the advisory board for the University of North Carolina-Greensboro undergraduate school of business and the advisory board of Discovery Learning. She can be contacted at saraking@optimuminsights.com.

DAVID G. ALTMAN is executive vice president of research, innovation, and product development at the Center for Creative Leadership. Previously he spent ten years as professor and associate professor of public health sciences and of pediatrics at the Wake Forest University School of Medicine in Winston-Salem, North Carolina, and ten years as a senior research scientist (and postdoctoral fellow and research associate) at Stanford University School of Medicine in Palo Alto, California. He has published over one hundred journal articles, book chapters, and books. He received his M.A. and Ph.D. degrees in social ecology from the University of California, Irvine, and his B.A. in psychology from the University of California, Santa Barbara. He has served as national program director of the Robert Wood Johnson Foundation (RWJF) Substance Abuse Policy Research Program, a $66 million, investigator-initiated research initiative. He has also served as conational program director of the RWJF Ladder to Leadership Program, a $4 million leadership development program for nonprofit leaders in health and health care and as conational program director of the RWJF Executive Nurse Fellows Program. In 1997, he was selected as one of forty Americans to participate in the three-year W. K. Kellogg Foundation National Leadership Program. David is a fellow of three divisions of the American Psychological Association and the Society of Behavioral Medicine. He is also a member of the American Public Health Association, Council on Epidemiology and Prevention of the American Heart Association, the Society of Public Health Education, and Academy of Behavioral Medicine Research. He can be contacted at altmand@ccl.org.

ABOUT THE CENTER FOR CREATIVE LEADERSHIP

The Center for Creative Leadership (CCL) is a top-ranked, global provider of executive education that unlocks individual and organizational potential through its exclusive focus on leadership education and research. Founded in 1970 as a nonprofit educational institution, CCL helps clients worldwide cultivate creative leadership—the capacity to achieve more than imagined by thinking and acting beyond boundaries—through an array of programs, products, and other services.

CCL ranked number 3 overall in the 2010 *Financial Times* worldwide survey of executive education and was ranked in the top 5 by *BusinessWeek* in 2009. It is headquartered in Greensboro, North Carolina, with campuses in Colorado Springs, Colorado; San Diego, California; Brussels, Belgium; and Singapore; and with offices in several cities in India and in Moscow, Russia, and Addis Ababa, Ethiopia. Supported by more than 450 faculty members and staff, it works annually with more than twenty thousand leaders and two thousand organizations. In addition, fourteen Network Associates around the world offer selected CCL programs and assessments.

CCL draws strength from its nonprofit status and educational mission, which provide unusual flexibility in a world where quarterly profits often drive thinking and direction. It has the freedom to be objective, wary of short-term trends, and motivated foremost by its mission—hence, its substantial and sustained investment in leadership research. Although CCL's work is always grounded in a strong foundation of research, it focuses on achieving a beneficial impact in the real world. Its efforts are geared to be practical and action oriented, helping leaders and their organizations more effectively achieve their goals and vision. The desire to transform learning and ideas into action provides the impetus for CCL's programs, assessments, publications, and services.

Capabilities

CCL's activities encompass leadership education, knowledge generation and dissemination, and building a community centered on leadership. CCL is broadly recognized for excellence in executive education, leadership development, and innovation by sources such as *BusinessWeek, Financial Times, Forbes,* the *Washington Post,* the *New York Times,* and the *Wall Street Journal.*

Open-Enrollment Programs

Fifteen open-enrollment courses are designed for leaders at all levels, as well as people responsible for leadership development and training at their organizations. This portfolio offers distinct choices for participants seeking a particular learning environment or type of experience. Some programs are structured specifically around small group activities, discussion, and personal reflection, while others offer hands-on opportunities through business simulations, artistic exploration, team-building exercises, and new-skills practice. Many of these programs offer private one-on-one sessions with a feedback coach.

For a complete listing of open-enrollment programs and the Leader Development Roadmap, visit http://www.ccl.org/leadership/programs/index.aspx.

Customized Programs

CCL develops tailored educational solutions for more than one hundred client organizations around the world each year. Through this applied practice, CCL structures and delivers programs focused on specific leadership development needs within the context of defined organizational challenges, including innovation, the merging of cultures, and the development of a broader pool of leaders. The objective is to help organizations develop, within their own cultures, the leadership capacity they need to address challenges as they emerge.

Program details are available at http://www.ccl.org/leadership/solutions/index.aspx.

Coaching

CCL's suite of coaching services is designed to help leaders maintain a sustained focus and generate increased momentum toward achieving their goals. These coaching alternatives vary in depth and duration and serve a variety of needs, from helping an executive sort through career and life issues to working with an organization to integrate coaching into its internal development process. CCL's coaching offerings, which can supplement program attendance or be customized for specific individual or team needs, are based on its model of assessment, challenge, and support (ACS).

Learn more about CCL's coaching services at http://www.ccl.org/leadership/coaching/index.aspx.

Assessment and Development Resources

CCL pioneered 360-degree feedback and believes that assessment provides a solid foundation for learning, growth, and transformation and that development truly happens when an individual recognizes the need to change. CCL offers a broad selection of assessment tools, online resources, and simulations that can help individuals, teams, and organizations increase their self-awareness, facilitate their own learning, enable their development, and enhance their effectiveness.

CCL's assessments are profiled at http://www.ccl.org/leadership/assessments/index.aspx.

Publications

The theoretical foundation for many of CCL's programs, as well as the results of its extensive and often groundbreaking research, can be found in the scores of publications issued by CCL Press and through the center's alliance with Jossey-Bass, a Wiley imprint. Among these are landmark works, such as *Breaking the Glass Ceiling* and *The Lessons of Experience,* as well as quick-read guidebooks focused on core aspects of leadership. CCL publications provide insights and practical advice to help individuals become more effective leaders, develop leadership training within organizations, address issues of change and diversity, and build the systems and strategies that advance leadership collectively at the institutional level.

A complete listing of CCL publications is available at http://www.ccl.org/leadership/publications/index.aspx.

Leadership Community

To ensure that its work remains focused, relevant, and important to the individuals and organizations it serves, CCL maintains a host of networks, councils, and learning and virtual communities that bring together alumni, donors, faculty, practicing leaders, and thought leaders from around the globe. CCL also forges relationships and alliances with individuals, organizations, and associations that share its values and mission. The energy, insights, and support from these relationships help shape and sustain CCL's educational and research practices and provide its clients with an added measure of motivation and inspiration as they continue their lifelong commitment to leadership and learning.

To learn more, visit http://www.ccl.org/leadership/community/index.aspx.

Research

CCL's portfolio of programs, products, and services is built on a solid foundation of behavioral science research. The role of research at CCL is to advance the understanding of leadership and transform learning into practical tools for participants and clients. CCL's research is the hub of a cycle that transforms knowledge into applications and applications into knowledge, thereby illuminating the way organizations think about and enact leadership and leader development.

Find out more about current research initiatives at http://www.ccl.org/leadership/research/index.aspx.

For additional information about CCL, visit http://www.ccl.org or call Client Services at 336-545-2810.